Career Compass
A Guide to Career Exploration
Vicky Payne

VP CRC, LLC

Published by **VP CRC, LLC**, doing business as **VP Career Exploration**
Overland Park, Kansas
vpcareerexploration.com

First edition, 2025
Printed in the United States of America

Contents

Chapter One

Philosophy & Method

Embarking on the journey of career exploration is a deeply personal process, and this book is designed to help you navigate that journey with clarity, intention, and purpose. Whether you're a high school student about to graduate, a college-age young adult contemplating your next step, or an adult in transition, this process can benefit anyone who is uncertain about their career path, seeking to change directions, or feeling stuck in their current role.

This book isn't just about crafting a career plan or finding your next step in isolation—it does both. It recognizes that career decisions are complex and multifaceted, shaped by both immediate needs and long-term aspirations.

The world of work has changed dramatically in recent decades, and with it, the way we approach career exploration. You've likely been asked, "What do you want to be when you grow up?"—a simple question when you were a child, but one that becomes much more difficult to answer as you grow older. Society often pressures us to choose a career path early on, but the reality is that few of us fully understand all the nuances involved in making such a choice without engaging in thoughtful exploration.

Your career will influence nearly every aspect of your life, from your personal well-being to your professional fulfillment. It's not just about a paycheck or a title—it's about finding alignment between your work, strengths, interests, values, and goals. This book understands that making career decisions is rarely straightforward, and that's why it walks you through a simple, yet strategic four-part process. This framework will help you assess yourself and different careers, ultimately leading you to discover a path that matches you.

FOUR-PART CAREER EXPLORATION PROCESS

Part 1 – Understand Yourself

The first step in choosing a fulfilling career is understanding who you are. What are your strengths, interests, values, goals, biases, personality traits, etc.? Before you can make a decision about your career, you need to know where you're starting from—what drives you, what excites you, and what you want from your professional life.

Part 2 – Additional Considerations

Your career decision shouldn't be made without considering all the variables and circumstances in your life. Your personal goals, responsibilities, and current situation will all play a crucial role in shaping your path. It's important to evaluate practical factors like location, work-life balance, compensation, and job stability—along with other considerations—before making any final decisions.

Part 3 - Explore Options

Once you've gained clarity on who you are and your personal circumstances, the next step is exploring the career possibilities available to you. This isn't just about looking up job listings or asking people for career advice. It's about deeply researching career fields, evaluating options, and being open to opportunities you may not have considered. The more you research and learn, the better informed your decision will be. And while it may be tempting to start your career exploration by focusing on income or salary, I challenge you to wait until Part 3 of the process. The all-important consideration of income should come after understanding yourself and your personal circumstances.

Part 4 - Create a Plan

After completing the first three parts of this process, it's time to put everything together and create a concrete, actionable plan. This plan will outline the steps you need to take to achieve your career goals, from the education and experience required, to the professional connections you need to make, and the skills you must develop. A clear plan not only keeps you focused and motivated but also increases the likelihood of successfully achieving your ultimate goal. By ensuring that all the elements of your career exploration are aligned with your personal, education, and work life, you'll be better positioned to take strategic, purposeful steps toward your desired career path.

EXPLORATION REQUIRES SELF-REFLECTION

Career exploration is not just about looking at job titles and finding one that sounds appealing. It includes self-discovery. You need to understand who you are before you decide who you want to become. Your interests, your skills, and your personality traits will all play a crucial role in shaping your career. This book will guide you through a series of introspective exercises to help you understand yourself on a deeper level, so that you can make a decision that is right for you—not what someone else wants or expects from you.

Understanding your personal circumstances is just as important. You might have financial constraints, family obligations, or other responsibilities that can impact your career decision. Taking the time to think about these factors will help you make a more informed and realistic choice.

Be Open to Possibilities

As you explore career options, keep an open mind. You might be surprised by what you find. A career that you never considered before may turn out to be a great fit for you. Exploring your options involves research and reflection. Be prepared to evaluate different possibilities, whether they are related to your current skills or completely new areas of interest.

By fully researching these factors, you will be able to assess for yourself which careers are a good, or great, fit for you and your goals. Your "Maybe List" will grow as you discover possibilities you hadn't previously considered.

Making the Final Decision

At some point, you'll need to make a decision. This can feel overwhelming, but the goal of this book is to help you weigh your options and make an informed choice. Explore multiple scenarios, reflect on the possibilities, and imagine what each path could look like in real life. Then, create a plan with clear steps that will help you achieve your goal. Having a SMART plan—Specific, Measurable, Achievable, Relevant, and Time-bound—will give you the structure you need to stay on track and motivated.

Remember, career exploration isn't a quick fix—it's a journey. It may take time, and you may encounter unexpected challenges along the way. Be prepared to adapt your plan as life changes, and remain flexible enough to pivot when needed.

Why Career Exploration is Personal

This process is yours, and only yours. No one else can do this for you—not your parents, your teachers, or even a computer program. Career choices are influenced by a vast number of factors, from the job market and economy to your interests, abilities, and personal circumstances. You are the only person truly qualified to make these decisions. It's important to take full ownership of your career exploration journey.

The work you do now—self-reflection, research, and planning—will lay the foundation for a fulfilling and successful career. What you discover during this process will not only impact your immediate future, but also help you navigate your career for years to come. By investing time and effort into this process, you are making a long-term investment in yourself. As you progress through your career journey, the skills and insights you gain will help you make informed decisions and adjustments when necessary. Life and work circumstances will inevitably change, and having a clear understanding of your strengths, interests, values, goals, and personal circumstances will empower you to adapt and stay on track.

CAREER COMPASS WORKBOOK

While the exercises and activities in this book can be completed without the *Career Compass Workbook*, having a dedicated space to record your thoughts, insights, and research can be invaluable. The workbook provides a structured place for reflection, exercises, and some additional activities that will guide you more deeply through the career exploration process. If you'd like to enhance your experience, you can purchase a digital or paper copy of the workbook at <u>vpcareerexploration.com</u>.

As you move forward, keep in mind that career exploration is not a one-time event. It's an ongoing process that will continue to evolve as you grow and change. So, take the time now to engage fully with the exercises in this book, and allow the exploration to unfold.

Author's Note

If you're seeking career help because you need to find a job quickly due to financial pressures or personal circumstances, please understand that your situation may require more immediate action. The advice in this book is intended for those who have the time and flexibility to take a more strategic approach to employment, which might not be an option for you right now. If that's the case, prioritize securing a job as soon as possible. Once you're able, you can revisit this material and take the time to plan your next steps.

Chapter Two

Message to Parents & Well-Intentioned Loved Ones

Once again, career exploration is a deeply personal journey. It's about self-discovery, growth, and the process of finding a path that truly aligns with one's strength, interests, values, and goals. As much as we want to help our loved ones navigate this process, it's crucial to understand that the responsibility for exploring and ultimately deciding on a career path rests with the individual. While your support and encouragement are vital, career exploration can only be effective when it's driven by the person who will live that career. This chapter is intended to guide you in offering the right kind of support—one that fosters independence, builds confidence, and creates an environment in which your loved one feels empowered to make their own decisions.

Career Exploration is Personal

The first and most important point to recognize is that career exploration is a personal process. Your loved one is the one who needs to engage with the material, answer the questions, and reflect on the exercises in this book. They are the ones who need to dig deep and figure out what truly excites them, what aligns with their skills, and what they are willing to pursue long term. As much as you may want to step in and take charge, this journey can only be transformative if it's led by the person doing the exploration. Think of it like helping someone navigate a new city—though you may know the streets well and have valuable advice, the other person must walk the path themselves to truly understand it, make it their own, and succeed on their journey, even if you're not by their side.

LET THEM OWN THEIR DECISIONS

It's only natural for you to want what's best for your loved one. You want them to be successful, independent, and able to navigate life's challenges confidently. You want them to choose a career that will give them stability, fulfillment, and financial security. However, career exploration is not about imposing your vision for their future—it's about helping them find their own. This process can't be forced, and it certainly can't be rushed. It must come from within them, fueled by their own curiosity and desire to find something that excites them.

Allow them to make their own decisions. This may feel uncomfortable, especially when you think they are making mistakes or take longer than you would expect or hope. But that's okay! Mistakes are part of the learning process, and it's important for them to experience them in order to build confidence and resilience. This is their career journey, and they must own it. They need the space to figure out what they want, even if they change their minds multiple times. Allowing them to explore freely, without the pressure of meeting your expectations, will help them come to their own conclusions and move forward with a greater sense of purpose, autonomy, and confidence.

This might be hard to hear and difficult advice to accept, but it's important to allow natural consequences to unfold rather than stepping in with punishment or rescuing your loved one if this process does not go as expected. Consequences are how people learn; punishment is about control. When you try to enforce punitive measures, you may feel that you're teaching an important or necessary life lesson, but this approach often leads to resentment and frustration. While consequences are a natural result of choices, punishment is a forced response, typically driven by a desire to exert control over the situation. Over time, these attempts to control can backfire, breaking trust and fostering a sense of rebellion rather than growth. You might think you're helping by preventing mistakes, but in reality what you are doing is shielding yourself from the discomfort of seeing your loved one struggle. In doing so, you are denying them the invaluable opportunity to learn and grow from their actions.

This isn't about success or failure—it's about success or learning, and both are valuable outcomes. By allowing your loved one the space to experience consequences instead of rescuing them, you provide them with the opportunity to develop resilience, build confidence, and ultimately succeed on their own terms. However, it's also important to recognize that this process can, and should, require clear boundaries.

SETTING HEALTHY BOUNDARIES

Setting boundaries is an essential part of helping your loved one with their career exploration, both for you and for them. While your advice can be valuable, it's crucial to offer it only when asked. Hovering, pressuring, or pushing your loved one in a direction they're not ready to go will only create resistance and frustration. Instead, be available to listen, offer suggestions when invited, and provide support as they work through the exploration process.

One of the most challenging aspects of helping someone explore their career options is knowing when to step in and when to step back. There will be times when you feel tempted to intervene—perhaps when you believe they are making a poor decision or are stuck in indecision. This is where boundaries come in. It's important to know your role: you're there to support, not to control. Sometimes, the best thing you can do is offer a safe space for them to express their thoughts and fears, without judgment or immediate solutions. The more they feel empowered to make their own decisions, the more they will develop the confidence and self-awareness necessary to succeed in their chosen career path.

At the same time, it's important to have appropriate boundaries to ensure progress is being made. You don't want an adult child living with you indefinitely, without taking active steps toward progressing in their future. Giving them the time and space to discover their path is essential, but there should also be reasonable expectations in place. Encourage them to set goals and take tangible steps toward their career development, whether it's gaining experience, seeking education, or networking. Supporting them means balancing patience with accountability, ensuring they are moving forward, and making progress on their journey.

Here are some examples that may help you to understand how to set appropriate boundaries with your loved one:

Boundary: The career researcher must actively engage with the material and make progress in their career exploration.

Example: Designate a specific day and time to discuss

their career exploration progress. "Let's set a specific day and time each week to discuss your career exploration progress. I'm happy to support you, but let's establish some guidelines to ensure our time is productive. We'll set aside 60 minutes each week. I'd like to hear about what you've learned from the next section of *Career Compass*, as well as the exercises and research you've completed. During our discussion, I want to understand where I can offer support and guidance to help you move forward."

Boundary: Expect regular action toward career exploration.
Example: If your loved one is unsure about their career direction, encourage them to dedicate a certain number of hours each week to job searching, researching different careers, or taking online courses to build relevant skills. You might say, "I understand you're still figuring things out, but how about committing to spending five hours a week on researching careers or developing skills you're interested in? Let's check in each week to see how it's going."

One week later, you can ask, "What progress have you made this week on your career exploration?" This helps hold them accountable without doing the work for them. You're not stepping in to fix the situation; you're creating a space for them to take ownership of their journey.

If progress doesn't happen, it's essential to allow the natural consequence to unfold. For instance, if they continually choose not to take action, you might need to set a clear boundary, such as: "I've offered my support, but if you're not actively working on your career exploration, I can no longer provide X." And then follow through! This sets the expectation that their actions (or inactions) will directly affect the level of support you can offer.

(Hopefully, this is clear: this isn't about punishment or manipulation—it's about setting clear and realistic expectations. Your support is contingent upon their active participation. If they choose not to take the necessary steps toward career exploration, they will experience the natural consequence of a change in the level of your support. Over time, this will help them understand the importance of taking initiative and making progress on their own. By setting this kind of boundary, you give your loved one the space to learn from their decisions and take responsibility for their actions. It's not about being harsh; it's about empowering them to take ownership of their career path while also maintaining healthy boundaries that protect both of you.)

Boundary: Providing financial support only as a part of an actionable plan.
Example: If your loved one needs financial help while in between jobs or pursuing education, you might say, "I'm happy to help with expenses for a certain period of time, but I need to see that you're making progress toward your goals. Let's agree that you'll do X (in a specific time frame)."

THE ROLE OF PATIENCE & REALISTIC EXPECTATIONS

Patience is key during this professional process. Career exploration is not a quick process in which you select the first couple of industries or professions you come across—you need time to think, process, and reflect on the jobs, expectations, descriptions, and feedback from others to get a bigger picture. The job profession journey is just that—a journey which will most likely take longer than you anticipate. Your loved one may not understand your hesitancy, not jumping at a high-paying position, and appear uncertain, confused, or indecisive along the way, but that's part of the process. Understand that career decisions don't happen overnight. Realizing that this process is a marathon and not a sprint will help you to have realistic expectations.

It's also important to recognize that career exploration is not linear. There will be twists and turns, moments of clarity, and moments of doubt. You may feel one way, one day, and totally different toward that profession the next. Your loved one may change direction several times before feeling confident about their final decision—and that's perfectly normal. Career paths rarely follow a straight line, and changing directions is often an essential part of growth. Encourage them to embrace flexibility and give themselves permission to pivot when necessary. This is not failure; it's a sign of learning and progress. When all is said and done, the final choice is from the person who is pursuing the job in a specific industry.

Additionally, it's important to remember that young people's brains—especially the prefrontal cortex, which governs decision-making, impulse control, and long-term planning—are still developing. This means that making big decisions, like choosing a career, can be particularly challenging. Asking them to make life-altering educational and financial choices while still figuring out their sense of identity is not only difficult but also developmentally premature. Therefore, having realistic expectations and offering patient support is crucial during this time.

YOUR ROLE AS A SUPPORTIVE GUIDE

What is your role in all of this? You can be a supporter, but not their decision-maker. Your role is to provide encouragement, listen without judgment, and offer potential research, information, case studies and support when asked. Encourage them to take the time they need to explore their options, and remind them that it's okay to feel uncertain during the process. Be patient, be present, and resist the urge to impose your own desires or expectations on them. It's important that they feel this process is theirs to own. Shame or pressure will not lead to productive outcomes, so be mindful of creating a supportive environment where they can explore without fear of judgment.

And finally, remember that career exploration is about more than just finding a job—it's about discovering one's purpose, aligning personal values with career goals, and creating a fulfilling future. You are helping your loved one uncover not only their career path, but also a deeper sense of themselves.

This journey, though challenging at times, can strengthen your relationship and create lasting memories. As you work through this together, celebrate the milestones and the small victories, and remember that the process of self-discovery is just as important as the final destination.

Chapter Three

What's Required in Your Career Exploration

As you embark on the journey of career exploration, it's important to approach this process with a clear understanding of what is expected of you, what you will need to invest in this journey, and why it's worth every bit of time, effort, and energy you put into it. Career exploration is not a one-time decision or a quick fix—it's a comprehensive and often lengthy process that requires your active participation and commitment. This chapter will outline what you need to do, and how to prepare yourself for a successful, meaningful exploration.

HARD WORK, SELF REFLECTION & TIME

The process of career exploration will take time. It requires your focus, your dedication, and your active involvement. This is not something that you can outsource or rush through. While the exercises, assessments, and worksheets discussed in this book will guide you, the real work comes from within you. You must be ready to take a deep dive into your strengths, interests, values, goals, and personal circumstances. You will need to reflect on your past experiences and your current passions. This is not the time to rush through the material or give cursory answers—this process requires honesty, self-reflection, and an open mind.

A successful career exploration process requires more than just completing career assessments or reading this book. It requires that you engage with the material thoughtfully, honestly, and with intention. It requires self-reflection and, at times, uncomfortable introspection. You may find yourself confronting things about your past choices, your limitations, or your fears. You might be forced to challenge old beliefs about what you "should" do or the expectations that others have placed on you—including the pressures of social norms, location, environmental, or regional expectations, which is all a part of growth. Look at the information, concerns and expectations of others, but in the end it is your choice. The profession you choose, is your choice. You are the one spending your lifetime, day by day, in this position.

As you work through the exercises in this book, take the time to go deeper than surface-level answers. Write down your thoughts, feelings, and questions as they arise. Use the space in the workbook to document your thoughts and ideas. This isn't about finding the "right" answer quickly—it's about uncovering insights about yourself that will guide you toward a career path that aligns with your authentic self.

Expect the process to take longer than you may think. It's common to feel frustrated or stuck at times, especially when you encounter obstacles or periods of uncertainty. Your career path may not become crystal clear right away, and that's okay. This is a journey of discovery, and discovery takes time. Your progress will not be linear, and you might find yourself questioning your choices or changing directions more than once. That's part of the process.

EXPECT UNCERTAINTY

It's natural to want clear, immediate answers. We live in a world where we're often told that answers should be fast and simple. However, career exploration typically doesn't follow that formula. There will be moments of clarity, and there will be moments of doubt. You might feel overwhelmed or unsure at times. But this uncertainty is not something to fear—it's an essential part of the process. Embrace it. The uncertainty is a sign that you're challenging yourself, thinking deeply about your future, and working toward a more meaningful career path.

You might go through several iterations of your career interests or change your mind multiple times before landing on something that truly resonates with you. Again, this is entirely normal. Career exploration is about discovering what fits best for you—not just in the present, but for your long-term growth. Your path is likely to change as you change. Be open to that flexibility and give yourself permission to pivot if necessary.

COMMITMENT TO THE PROCESS

You might be asking yourself, "Why should I invest so much time and energy into this? What's the end goal?" The truth is, career exploration is a lifelong process. The decisions you make today will impact your immediate future, but they will also shape your longer-term career trajectory. When you take the time to fully engage with the exercises, assessments, and reflective activities in this book, you are investing in yourself for the long term.

Career exploration is frequently described as a journey, and like any journey, it will have its ups and downs. The more committed you are to seeing this through, the more rewarding the process will be. Stay engaged. Do the work, even when it feels tedious or frustrating. Set aside regular time for this process and stay disciplined about completing the exercises and assessments. Your investment in this process will pay off now and in the future, as you will develop skills and insights that will continue to serve you throughout your professional life.

Your success in career exploration depends on you staying committed to the process. There will be moments when you want to give up, when the road feels unclear, or when you feel like you're not making any progress. During these times, remember why you started. The clearer sense of purpose, direction, and confidence you'll gain through this exploration will have a lasting impact on your personal and professional life. And the insights you gain now will continue to guide you as you move forward in your career—whether you stay in one career path for years or change directions many times over the course of your life.

It's important to remember that your career decisions should not be made by someone else for you. Don't delegate that responsibility to anyone else, including a computerized career assessment. There are simply too many unknowns—too many variables that can't be quantified or predicted. From shifting labor markets and economic conditions to your unique interests, abilities, and skills, no one can fully understand your potential and aspirations the way you can. Yes, career assessments and insightful advice from others can provide clarity, but ultimately, you are the expert on yourself. You are the only one qualified to make these decisions.

This is your opportunity to define what success and fulfillment look like for you. Through this process, you will gain invaluable self-awareness that will not only in-form your career choices but will also help you make decisions in the future as your career continues to evolve. Your interests, skills, and values may change over time—and that's okay! The work you put in now will make it easier to adapt to those changes and approach your future with confidence and clarity.

At the end of the day, this is your journey. No one else can do the work for you. Your career exploration process requires your full participation and ownership. This process might not be easy—it is going to take time, effort, and patience. But every step you take now will bring you closer to discovering your true potential and to a career that aligns with who you are.

By fully committing to this process, embracing the challenges, and remaining patient with yourself, you will set yourself up for long-term success—not just in choosing a career, but in understanding yourself and navigating your career throughout your lifetime. Your career is a reflection of you—it's your path, your choices, and your future. Take this time and process seriously. Invest in yourself. The rewards will be worth it!

Get to Work

Now that you understand the importance of taking re-sponsibility for your career exploration, it's time to get started! This is your opportunity to define your future, and it requires active involvement and a commitment to face the challenges ahead. No one else can do this work for you. With each step, you'll gain insights and clarity that you'll need to move forward.

So, grab your Career Exploration Workbook (available at vpcareerexploration.com), or a notebook/some paper, and *get ready to work!*

Check-in

Are you ready to fully engage in this process and invest the time and effort needed to explore your true potential? If so, let's get started—your future begins now!

Part 1 - Understand Yourself

Chapter Four

Your Story

Understanding your personal story is crucial because it will help you make informed and thoughtful career decisions for yourself. Many people, when considering their careers, might focus on practical factors like salary or the ease of obtaining a position. Others may prioritize power, prestige, or lifestyle. However, taking the time to understand yourself provides the self-awareness and insight needed to make choices that align with your true strengths and values. Gaining this understanding takes time, introspection, and a willingness to dig deeper into who you are.

You are one of a kind. You are unique. You are a sum of not just your personality and interests, but also a unique combination of the factors that have influenced your life up until this point in time. Understanding all of these factors, and the influences they have had on you, will help you effectively assess yourself and comprehend your personal identity.

You will want to consider and examine specific areas of your life story. These areas offer insights into factors that have contributed to the formation of your personal identity. They have shaped you throughout your life in constructing your opinions, ideas, and biases. Also, consider that these potential biases could hold an unconscious internal meaning which could present a relevance for you. All of these factors, to varying degrees, could have planted seeds in your mind regarding your personal identity. Grasping your personal identity is crucial because of how it affects your thoughts about your career identity.

Choosing a career is like selecting an identity that speaks volumes about who you are, often without needing words. Just as being an athlete, gamer, or artist reveals your passions and lifestyle, your career becomes a defining part of your personal identity. For example, choosing to be an educator reflects a commitment to knowledge and nurturing others' growth, while becoming a nurse embraces empathy and care. Similarly, an airline pilot symbolizes responsibility and precision, and a network architect represents innovation and technical expertise. Your career not only shapes how others see you but also reflects your personal strengths, interests, and values. Ultimately, it gives you the power to define the professional persona you wish to project.

As you go through this chapter (and workbook), keep in mind that some factors and variables will be more relevant to you than others—and that's perfectly normal. You might also notice some overlapping ideas or repetitions. That's a positive sign! Pay extra attention to those areas and give them thoughtful consideration.

Keep in mind that a full-time professional spends over 2,000 hours a year at their job. For most people, that's more time than they spend doing any other activity, including sleeping! Given the enormity of the time commitment your career will play in your life, it becomes even clearer how important it is to understand yourself and your personal identity. This way, you can factor all relevant variables into your decision-making process—variables that may significantly contribute to your happiness, well-being, and ulti-mately define your career identity—'I am a _____.'

Staying in a job that doesn't align with who you are can lead to dissatisfaction, frustration, and even depression. Take the time to explore your true self to ensure that the career path you choose will lead to a fulfilling future, bringing happiness, contentment, and a sense of success. While challenges—such as difficult projects, customers, managers, or colleagues—are inevitable, even in these moments, you'll find a deeper sense of contentment and joy in knowing you're on the right path and spending your time in a way that truly aligns with who you are.

Get Ready to Work!

As you read along, use the *Career Compass Workbook* to record and reflect on your thoughts and ideas (pages 1–5).

WHAT ARE YOU GOOD AT?

In our society, we're often discouraged from speaking positively about ourselves, as it can be seen as bragging or being conceited. Set that aside for a moment. Think about what you're truly good at. Where do you excel? What skills and strengths do you have? Be mindful not to confuse the question, "What are you talented at?" with the broader idea of identifying your strengths—there's a difference.

You might be good at things you're also talented in, such as athletics, complex problem-solving, or building relationships with strangers. These are indeed talents (or gifts). However, it's important to consider whether you actually enjoy these activities, even if they come easily and effortlessly to you.

You can be a talented athlete but derive no pleasure in practicing or competing in a sport.

You might be great at solving complex problems, doing so faster and more creatively than those around you. But the important question to ask yourself is: do you enjoy it? Does it bring you personal satisfaction and pleasure, or does it feel more like a chore?

You can be the person who can talk to anyone. You connect effortlessly with strangers. You can make people feel instantly connected and safe with you, then ask yourself if you truly enjoy the effort it takes to build and maintain those relationships? Or does it seem daunting, superficial, or unfulfilling?

When considering all the things that you are good at, also consider if you enjoy interactions and spending your time doing them. Do they make you feel strong and satisfied?

If constructing a list of things you are good at is difficult or uncomfortable for you, do not worry. You are normal! You are good at lots of things—you may just not recognize it, or find it difficult to articulate. Ask some people close to you—those who love you most—to tell you the areas where they see you thrive. Consider their responses. Which of these things create feelings of strength and joy for you?

WHAT ARE YOUR HOBBIES?

In your free time, if given a choice, what are the things you voluntarily choose to do? How you choose to spend your free time can provide clues to guide you in your career exploration. If you can figure out qualities, aspects, or recurring themes in what you enjoy, you can be cognizant of whether those translate into potential career choices.

Be careful when answering this question. You might spend your free time watching TV, browsing social media, or watching TikTok. Those might be what you use to decompress or pass the time. That is different from a hobby. Consider what activities you do in your free time that make you feel happy, invigorated, energized, and leave you with a feeling of satisfaction or pride after you've engaged in them.

You can take this question and, rather than just creating a list of hobbies, spend some additional time digging a little deeper. Consider not just what your hobby is, but what about that hobby invigorates you. What are the specific elements that appeal to you and keep your engagement? For example, if one of your hobbies is traveling, what is it about traveling that brings you joy? Is it researching new places, learning the history, or experiencing new cultures? If your hobby is being a sports spectator, what about watching sports brings you joy? Is it the competition, skills, strategies, or the camaraderie and being part of an entity where you find acceptance and belonging?

WHAT DO YOU VALUE?

Everyone has their own set of personal values. Whether you are aware of them or not, your personal values shape your life. They influence your relationships, determine your choice of city to live in, affect the relationships you invest in, and so much more! Your values will also come into play throughout your professional career.

Working at a job or being part of a career field that goes against your values can and will lead to frustration, unhappiness, discontentment, and possibly depression. It is essential to know your core values so that you can be conscientious of them during your career decision-making process.

Understanding your personal values will most likely change as you experience more life adventures. Ask yourself, what you value now as that may be different from what you will value in the future. You will evolve and change based on your life experiences and personal circumstances. Unless you have some special abilities, you probably cannot predict the future or what values you may hold later on in life. So consider only the here and now, and take the time to identify what values are most important to you. Recognize and acknowledge that there is no right or wrong when it comes to your values. Being honest with yourself about what matters most to you will help you more accurately evaluate your needs when considering career choices. Recognizing and honoring your core values will be important for you to consider throughout your professional career.

HOW DO YOU ENVISION YOUR FUTURE?

When you think of your future, what does it look like? What do you want? What kinds of things are most important to you—where you live, lifestyle, family, health, and/or free time? There is no right or wrong answer, and absolutely no need to feel self-conscious. Be honest with yourself and allow yourself to daydream about your ideal future. What are the different elements and key components of how you see your future? Spend some time thinking about how a career looks and fits into these potential future possibilities.

Get to Work

What new insights or understanding have you gained about who you are? (*Career Compass Workbook*, pages 1–5.)

- What are you good at?

- What are your hobbies?

- What do you value?

- How do you envision your future?

Check-in

You should have some notes by now to begin piecing together the story of you. You know what you are good at (your strengths), what you enjoy (your interests), what values matter most to you (your core values), and what you want your future to look like (your goals). This self-understanding is what you need to understand how you got to this point in your life. Know your story, understand it, and accept it for what it is! This is the beginning of the self-examination process that will provide you with an accurate starting point on your career exploration journey.

Chapter Five

External Influences & Biases

External influences and biases can shape, and even distort, your interpretation of your personal and career identity. Continue to examine your present starting point by considering what external factors and biases have influenced and shaped your thoughts and ideas, either consciously or unconsciously. Specifically, think about the external factors that influence your thoughts when it comes to making career choices. Consider potential factors and identify which ones influence you and how they manifest.

Often, our life story can create within us biases which can affect our career choices. It is incredibly common for these biases to be unconscious. Take some time to carefully consider your experiences, influences, and the ways they have shaped your thoughts and ideas about career choices.

Some of the potential factors that could influence your thoughts and ideas regarding career choices and decisions include culture, disability, gender, sexual identity, sexual orientation, parents, peers, religion, socioeconomic status, and trauma. Not all of these will be relevant to you, and there could be additional factors that apply specifically to you that are not included in this list. Do not discount anything that feels important and significant to you and your life experiences. Also, recognize that some of these factors may intersect with each other. Examine these intersections or redundancies and give those areas special attention when considering their influence on you. Consider what factors may have affected you and how they have shaped your beliefs surrounding career choices.

Author's Note

I often find, while working with clients and students, that this portion of the process can be easy for them to breeze through with little thought or effort. I frequently receive reports that none of these variables have affected them and they eagerly want to move on to taking career assessments. I encourage you to take some time to think about your life and put effort into considering any and all external influences you might have experienced, as well as any conscious or unconscious biases that may have formed within you regarding career choices.

While this is not always the case, I find that the younger a client or student is, the fewer insights they can identify during this process. If, for any reason, you find this exercise difficult, I encourage you to work through this chapter with someone who knows a lot about you, your life, and your experiences. They might be able to offer insights you otherwise may not have considered or discovered about yourself.

Get Ready to Work!

As you read along, identify which external influences and biases have influenced and shaped your thoughts and ideas regarding education and career choices. Record your thoughts and ideas in the *Career Compass Workbook* (page 6).

CULTURE

Culture influences career choices in a number of ways. Culture refers to the community we live in and the values that the community (and we) hold. Broadly speaking, culture encompasses our ways of life, beliefs, and traditions that are passed down from generation to generation.

Geography, ethnicity, race, and religion can all influence the culture you experience. Culture can play a multifaceted role in shaping career choices by influencing our perceptions, values, aspirations, and opportunities. Recognizing and understanding the influence of your culture can help you make informed career decisions.

Below are several ways in which culture can influence career decisions. Consider the following possibilities and reflect on how culture may influence your education and career choices.

Norms & Expectations

Cultural norms can dictate what is considered acceptable or desirable in terms of career choices. In some cultures, certain professions may be highly esteemed or encouraged. Conversely, other professions may be stigmatized or discouraged. Because of this, cultural identity and heritage may influence career choices. Individuals may be drawn to careers that reflect their cultural heritage or allow them to celebrate and preserve their cultural identity. Cultural traditions and norms may create resistance to exploring alternative career choices. Individuals may feel pressure to adhere to traditional career paths or roles, even as societal norms evolve.

Family

Family influence can play a pivotal role in many cultures in shaping career choices. Cultural expectations regarding duty, respect, or obligations may influence individuals to pursue careers that align with family values or expectations. (See PARENTS.)

Status & Prestige

Cultural values around status and prestige may influence career choices, as certain professions may be associated with higher social standing. This can lead people to choose careers that their culture regards as epitomizing success. In some cultures, success may be equated with financial wealth or professional achievement, while in others, success may be defined by factors such as happiness, fulfillment, or contribution to society.

Education

Cultural attitudes toward education can influence career choices. In cultures that prioritize education and academic achievement, individuals may feel pressured to pursue careers that require higher levels of education or specialized skills.

Values

Cultural values and beliefs can shape a person's career aspirations and goals. For example, cultures that emphasize collectivism and community may prioritize careers that contribute to the greater good or serve the needs of the community. Communities and peer groups also play a significant role in shaping career choices. Cultural expectations within social circles may influence individuals to pursue careers that are traditional or valued within their community.

Cultural attitudes toward work-life balance can also influence career decisions. Cultures that prioritize leisure time and family commitments may lead individuals to seek careers that offer flexibility and balance between work and personal life. Additionally, individuals may choose careers that align with their religious or spiritual values, or they may seek vocations that allow them to integrate their faith into their work. (See RELIGION.)

DISABILITY

People with disabilities may experience unique challenges when it comes to employment. Disabilities may include physical, mental/psychiatric, intellectual, learning, developmental, behavioral, emotional, or sensory conditions. The effects of disabilities on career choices can vary based on the nature and severity of the disability, as well as personal circumstances. Having a disability might present challenges or limitations when seeking employment, during the hiring process, acclimating to a new work position, and/or in retaining employment. Many factors could affect your ideas about which career possibilities are suitable for you, depending on your disability.

While disabilities may present employment challenges, they can also foster resilience and creativity. People with disabilities contribute positively to many professions because of their unique perspectives. Special consideration should be given to any functional limitations, physical restrictions, or other impediments when it comes to career choices. It is important to remember that in the United States, employers are required to provide reasonable accommodations to employees with disabilities. An employer cannot refuse to hire you because your disability prevents you from performing duties that are not essential to the job. Essential functions are the fundamental job duties that you must be able to perform, either on your own or with the help of a reasonable accommodation. It is imperative to know your rights and the laws protecting people with disabilities in the workplace and to be prepared to advocate for yourself.

Below are several ways in which a disability can influence career decisions. Consider the following possibilities and reflect on how a disability may influence your education or career choices.

Physical Limitations

Individuals with physical disabilities may face challenges related to mobility, dexterity, or stamina. This can influence the types of professions and work environments a person may consider in order to accommodate their physical abilities or for safety reasons.

Hidden Disabilities

Individuals with hidden disabilities may face additional struggles, as their conditions are not immediately apparent, often leading to misunderstandings, lack of accommodations, or biases during the job search and work life. Overcoming these barriers may require extra self-advocacy, awareness, and seeking out supportive work environments that prioritize inclusivity and flexibility.

Accessible Work Environment

A person with a disability may prioritize professions or employers known for providing inclusive and accessible work environments. This can include the availability of assistive technology and adaptive equipment necessary to accommodate their specific needs. Having an accessible work environment may require special consideration when a person needs to transition between careers due to changing needs and abilities, in order to accommodate evolving circumstances.

Education Opportunities

Some careers may have educational requirements that pose additional challenges for individuals with certain disabilities, while others may be more accessible. This may discourage or encourage consideration of certain careers. Access to training programs and skill development opportunities is essential for career advancement. Individuals with disabilities may gravitate toward professions that provide accessible training and ongoing skill development.

Discrimination

Concerns regarding discrimination, or stigma related to disabilities, can influence career choices and cause individuals to avoid certain professions or workplaces due to concerns about potential bias or limited opportunities for advancement. It may feel more appealing to seek a profession where anti-discrimination protections and workplace accommodations are well-established.

Mental Health

Career choices may be limited in order to prioritize mental health needs, social and emotional well-being, and a healthy work-life balance. Individuals with disabilities may seek roles that offer a supportive and understanding environment. They may prioritize professions that contribute positively to their overall life satisfaction and well-being.

Remote Work & Self Employment

The flexibility of work arrangements, including remote work options, can be appealing and sometimes necessary for individuals with disabilities. Certain careers that offer flexibility in work hours and locations may be more attractive. Additionally, people with disabilities often consider exploring entrepreneurship or self-employment, as it allows for greater flexibility in accommodating individual needs and preferences.

Advocacy & Social Impact

Due to personal experiences, individuals with disabilities may be drawn to careers involving advocacy, social impact, or working with organizations focused on disability rights. This allows them to contribute to positive change and support others facing similar challenges. There is often a strong appeal to pursue a career that aligns with personal passions and values.

Finances

Financial considerations, including disability benefits, healthcare costs, and the need for additional support services, may require special consideration when exploring career choices. This ensures stability and access to necessary benefits.

Community & Networking

Individuals with disabilities may be drawn to professions where they find a supportive community or where colleagues share similar experiences. They may seek professions with access to a network that helps them navigate potential workplace or professional challenges. Networking and mentorship opportunities can provide exposure, support, and potential opportunities for career growth.

GENDER

Gender can have a profound impact on an individual's career choices due to societal expectations, stereotypes, and structural barriers. Men and women may have undergone different socialization experiences throughout their lives. Based on gender, they may have been treated differently and held to different standards by teachers, guidance counselors, coaches, parents, bosses, and others. This can influence beliefs about what career opportunities are suitable based on gender. While significant progress has been made in promoting gender equality in the workplace, challenges still exist. Efforts to promote gender equality, challenge stereotypes, and address structural barriers help create environments where individuals can make career choices based on their interests, skills, and aspirations, rather than predetermined gender norms.

Below are several ways in which gender can influence career decisions. Consider the following possibilities and reflect on how gender may influence your education and career choices.

Expectations & Stereotypes

Traditional gender norms can influence people to consider or avoid certain professions based on perceived appropriateness. Certain industries and occupations are perceived as "male-dominated" or "female-dominated," with women and men concentrated in different fields. These gendered perceptions may limit consideration of certain professions. Stereotypes exist about the compatibility of specific genders with particular industries, which can also impact career choices. Cultural and societal norms regarding gender roles can shape perceptions of what is considered acceptable. Gender-based barriers, often referred to as the "glass ceiling," can limit professional advancement for women. The perception that certain leadership roles are more suitable for men can also impact career aspirations.

Education

Gender can influence educational choices, with some fields of study traditionally associated with specific genders. Stereotypes about "women's" or "men's" fields may impact the academic paths a person chooses. For example, in science, technology, engineering, and mathematics (STEM) fields, there are gender imbalances that can influence both education and career choices.

Wage Gap

The gender wage gap—where women earn less than men for similar work—can influence career decisions. Women may consider factors such as potential earnings and financial stability when choosing a career.

Work-Life Balance/Impacts on Parenthood

Parenthood can have different impacts on men's and women's careers. Parents (or future parents) may want or need to consider the potential effects of parenthood on their career progression and may make career choices influenced by family planning. Gender roles and expectations regarding caregiving responsibilities can influence decisions related to work-life balance. Both men and women may consider professions that offer flexibility and can accommodate family responsibilities.

Representation

Unequal access to leadership training and development opportunities can impact career trajectories. Women may encounter barriers to acquiring the skills and experiences necessary for advancement. Limited representation of women in leadership positions may also affect career aspirations. The absence of visible role models in certain industries can shape a person's perception of their potential for career growth in those fields.

Discrimination

Women may be more likely to face challenges in being perceived as competent or confident, which can impact career choices and opportunities. Gender-based discrimination and biases can affect career decisions. Individuals may be dissuaded from pursuing certain careers due to concerns about facing discrimination or bias in the workplace. The #MeToo movement has increased awareness of workplace harassment issues, which may also influence career choices. Some individuals may consider workplace culture and the potential for harassment when making career decisions.

Networking

Gender differences in networking opportunities can impact career choices. Women may face challenges in accessing influential networks or mentorship, which can affect career advancement and opportunities.

GENDER IDENTITY & SEXUAL ORIENTATION

People who identify as Lesbian, Gay, Bisexual, Transgender, Queer, Intersex, Asexual, and other identities (LGBTQIA+) can face unique challenges in career selection and the labor market because of their sexual identity and/or sexual orientation. Individuals who identify as LGBTQIA+ frequently express caution, concern, and/or apprehension when exploring and selecting a post-secondary education institution, college major, or career path. These choices may feel limited due to concerns that certain industries might support or inhibit their ability to present themselves authentically in the workplace. These concerns and feelings are shaped by societal attitudes, workplace environments, legal protections, and personal factors. Encouraging diversity, equity, and inclusion across all industries can contribute to more inclusive and fulfilling career opportunities for everyone. It is essential to recognize the diversity within the LGBTQIA+ community, as individuals may have unique experiences and considerations based on their specific identities and circumstances. As societal attitudes continue to evolve and workplaces become more inclusive, those who identify as LGBTQIA+ will hopefully find greater opportunities for fulfilling and supportive career paths of their choosing.

Below are several ways in which sexual orientation and gender identity can influence career decisions. Consider the following possibilities and reflect on how gender identity and sexual orientation may influence your education and career choices.

Discrimination & Bias

People who identify as LGBTQIA+ may face discrimination and bias in the workplace, which can impact career choices and opportunities. Concerns about potential discrimination can influence decisions related to disclosing one's identity and selecting inclusive workplaces. Legal protections against discrimination based on sexual orientation and gender identity vary across regions and countries. The presence or absence of legal protections can affect the comfort and security LGBTQIA+ individuals feel when pursuing certain careers. The availability of inclusive policies and benefits—such as non-discrimination policies, healthcare coverage, and family leave—can also influence career decisions. Individuals may prioritize workplaces that offer these supportive policies.

Education

Educational choices, including the selection of majors and fields of study, can be influenced by LGBTQIA+ identity. Identifying as LGBTQIA+ may also impact career choices in fields like the arts and creative industries. These professions may offer opportunities for self-expression and storytelling related to LGBTQIA+ experiences. Some individuals may pursue academic paths aligned with their advocacy interests or community involvement.

Visibility & Representation

The visibility and representation of LGBTQIA+ individuals in various professions can influence career decisions. Seeing successful LGBTQIA+ role models can inspire individuals and contribute to a sense of belonging in specific fields.

Supportive Environment

The presence of supportive and inclusive work environments can positively impact career choices. People who identify as LGBTQIA+ may be more likely to pursue careers in workplaces that prioritize diversity, equity, and inclusion. Some individuals may prioritize workplaces where they feel comfortable being open about their identity, while others may prefer privacy and seek environments with fewer disclosure expectations. Identifying as LGBTQIA+ may lead individuals to pursue careers in advocacy, activism, or organizations that focus on LGBTQIA+ rights. Some individuals may be drawn to professions that allow them to contribute to positive societal change. Career trajectory and advancement opportunities can also be influenced by the workplace climate. Some people may experience barriers to career progression, while others may find supportive environments that foster professional growth. The impact of identifying as LGBTQIA+ on workplace relationships is significant. The quality of relationships with colleagues, supervisors, and clients can influence job satisfaction and career decisions.

Mental Health/Well-Being

The mental health and well-being of LGBTQIA+ individuals can be influenced by workplace climates. Hostile environments or a lack of support may lead individuals to prioritize mental health and overall well-being when making career choices. Considerations of work-life balance may also be influenced by LGBTQIA+ identity. People may seek professions or workplaces that offer flexibility and accommodation for personal life, including relationships and family responsibilities.

Networking & Mentorship

Networking and mentorship opportunities can be influenced by one's LGBTQIA+ identity. Supportive networks and mentorship are crucial for career advancement, and individuals may seek environments that provide these opportunities. The presence of social support networks within and outside the workplace can influence career decisions. People who identify as LGBTQIA+ may prioritize environments where they can connect with supportive communities and allies.

PARENTS

Parents can have a significant influence on their children's career choices, shaping their attitudes, values, and aspirations. Several factors contribute to the impact parents have on their children's career decisions. It is important to note that while parents can have a substantial impact, children are individuals with their own interests, strengths, and preferences. The ideal approach is a balanced one that considers both parental guidance and the child's unique qualities and aspirations. Open communication, support, and encouragement can contribute to a positive influence on a child's career journey.

It's also important to note that parental influence is not limited to childhood; even adult children can still be deeply affected by their parents' opinions and expectations when making career decisions.

Below are several ways in which parents can influence career decisions. Consider the following possibilities and how parents may influence your education and career choices.

Modeling

Parents serve as primary role models for their children. Throughout a child's lifetime, parents model what is considered normal, appropriate, and acceptable. The careers and work habits of parents can influence a child's perception of various professions and work ethics. Parents set an example for their children through their life choices. Observing their work-life balance can shape a child's expectations and priorities regarding their future career. Balancing work and personal life is often a learned behavior.

Education Expectations

Many parents have specific expectations for their children's education, career, and life choices. Parents' expectations regarding education play a crucial role in shaping a child's approach to learning and career aspirations. The emphasis on academic achievement and the value placed on education can influence a child's commitment to learning and pursuing higher education. Parents can reinforce this by providing opportunities for their children to learn and develop. Attitudes toward higher education or vocational training can also impact a child's thoughts and decisions regarding education and career choices.

Values

Cultural and family values may significantly impact career choices. The values held by the family, extended family, and family friends reflect beliefs about work, success, and fulfillment. These values can shape a child's understanding of what constitutes a desirable or meaningful career.

Support & Encouragement

A parent's financial situation can impact a child's career choices. Additionally, the financial resources made available by parents to support and encourage certain endeavors can significantly influence a child's career path. Positive reinforcement, encouragement, and support from parents can boost a child's confidence in pursuing their interests and goals. Conversely, the lack of financial support or the withholding of resources may hinder the exploration of certain career paths.

Advice

Open and effective communication between parents and children facilitates discussions about career interests, goals, and concerns. Supportive communication allows children to express themselves and seek guidance. Parents' expectations regarding their children's career paths can create pressure or provide motivation. Children may feel compelled to choose careers that align with parental expectations, even if those expectations are not explicitly stated. Parents often provide educational guidance, such as helping with subject choices, discussing college options, and guiding career-related decisions throughout the education process. Parents also offer career counseling based on their own experiences, sharing insights and advice that can provide valuable support. The level of involvement parents have in their children's decision-making processes can influence a child's sense of autonomy and their confidence in making decisions.

Exposure

The exposure that children have to their parents' professions or to various careers within the family or social circle can influence their awareness and understanding of different job opportunities. The parents' occupations directly influence a child's exposure to specific industries. Children are more likely to consider careers in fields related to their parents' professions, as parents can provide professional networks, opportunities, or connections in those industries.

Gender Roles

Parents may have expectations regarding gender roles and career choices that can influence the career paths their children perceive as acceptable or desirable. (See GENDER.)

Culture

Cultural norms and expectations within the family's cultural background can play a significant role in shaping career choices. Cultural influences can impact career preferences and priorities. (See CULTURE.)

PEERS

The peers you socialize with can have a significant impact on your career choices. Often, career and education choices reflect those of our peers. People frequently look to their peers to validate their education and career decisions. Peers offer advice, encouragement, and validation. They can influence career choices because of shared lifestyles, cultures, values, behaviors, and education choices or opportunities. Social interactions and peer dynamics play a crucial role in shaping individual perceptions, preferences, and aspirations.

Below are several ways in which peers can influence career decisions. Consider the following possibilities and how peers may influence your education and career choices.

Norms & Expectations

Individuals may be influenced by the norms and expectations within their peer group. The prevailing attitudes toward certain professions or career paths can shape one's own perceptions and choices. Conversations with peers about career options, experiences, and aspirations can provide valuable insights. Peer advice and shared experiences can influence decisions and contribute to the exploration of different career paths. Close friendships and social connections can significantly affect career choices. Individuals may be drawn to professions or industries where their friends work, fostering a sense of camaraderie and shared experiences.

Comparison

Social comparison with peers can impact career choices. Individuals may be influenced by the perceived success or satisfaction of their peers in specific professions, leading them to consider similar paths. Healthy competition among peers can drive individuals to set ambitious career goals and pursue success. The desire to excel in comparison to peers may influence choices related to education, training, and career paths.

Support/Pressure

Peer support and encouragement can boost confidence and motivation. Positive reinforcement from peers may inspire individuals to pursue certain career goals or take risks in their professional endeavors. Peer networks provide access to professional connections and opportunities.

Individuals may learn about job openings, internships, or career events through their peers, which can impact their career decisions. Positive experiences of collaboration and teamwork with peers in academic or extracurricular settings can influence career choices. The sense of fulfillment derived from working with others may impact preferences for team-oriented professions.

Exploring career options together with peers can make the process more enjoyable and less daunting. Collaborative exploration and discussions may lead individuals to consider professions they hadn't previously explored. Peer mentorship can be influential in career decisions. Learning from the experiences of more experienced peers can guide individuals in making informed choices about education, internships, and career paths. Recognition and validation from peers for certain skills or achievements can impact career choices. Individuals may be motivated to pursue careers where their abilities are acknowledged and valued by their peers. Peer pressure can influence career decisions, as individuals may feel compelled to conform to the expectations or preferences of their peer group. This can affect choices related to majors, industries, or job preferences.

Exposure

Interacting with a diverse group of peers exposes individuals to different perspectives, values, and career experiences. Exposure to diverse viewpoints may broaden one's understanding of career possibilities. Observing the career experiences and mistakes of peers can serve as a learning opportunity. Individuals may adjust their own career decisions based on the successes or challenges faced by their peers. Observing the skill development and expertise of peers may inspire individuals to pursue similar paths. Peer influence can also shape decisions about acquiring specific skills and knowledge.

Commonalities

Shared interests and hobbies among peers can impact career choices. Individuals may be drawn to professions related to activities they enjoy with their friends, creating a sense of alignment between personal and professional life. Cultural and social trends within a peer group can influence career decisions. Emerging trends, such as preferences for certain industries or work arrangements, may shape individual choices. Peer values and priorities can also affect one's perspective on work-life balance and job satisfaction.

RELIGION

Religion can have a profound impact on an individual's values, beliefs, and worldview, influencing various aspects of life, including career choices. Religion can influence career interests and values. Religion may also be a source of academic study if your faith sponsors or encourages attending religious schools. Certain career pursuits may be more encouraged or discouraged based on religious beliefs. Some people may even view their career not merely as a choice but as a divine "calling." For instance, some religious individuals consider their talents to be gifts from a higher power, which must be utilized professionally to honor or glorify God.

The effects of religion on career decisions can be diverse, and it is important to recognize that the impact of religion on career choices is highly individual. Different religious traditions and personal interpretations within those traditions can lead to diverse influences on career decisions. People should aim to find a balance between their religious beliefs, personal interests, skills, and societal influences when making career choices.

Below are several ways in which religion can influence career decisions. Consider the following possibilities and how religion may influence your education and career choices.

Values

Religious beliefs can shape an individual's values and ethical framework, influencing the types of careers and industries that align with their moral and ethical principles. Religious traditions often emphasize certain principles and values. People may aspire to leadership roles in their careers, guided by religious teachings on responsibility, humility, and ethical leadership. Some religious traditions may impose restrictions on certain professions or industries. For example, individuals may avoid careers that conflict with specific religious teachings or tenets of their faith.

Purpose/Calling

Religion can provide individuals with a sense of purpose and meaning in life, which may guide career choices. This sense of purpose might lead individuals to pursue professions that align with what they believe is their spiritual calling. Some religious individuals may believe in a vocational calling or divine guidance in their career decisions, leading them to choose professions that they feel are aligned with their spiritual purpose. Individuals with strong religious convictions may be drawn to counseling or pastoral careers, where they can provide spiritual guidance, support, and care for others.

Service

Many religious traditions emphasize the importance of service and helping others. People influenced by this value may be drawn to careers in social work, healthcare, education, or other fields focused on making a positive impact on the lives of others. Religion often emphasizes community and social responsibility. Individuals may choose careers that allow them to contribute to the well-being of their communities or address social issues. People may feel driven by a sense of duty, a desire to contribute to charitable endeavors, or a commitment to making a positive impact on the world.

Perspective

Some religious beliefs emphasize the importance of maintaining a balance between work and personal life. This can influence career choices, as individuals seek professions that align with their desired work-life balance. Religious teachings may also promote cultural sensitivity and understanding. Individuals influenced by these teachings may be drawn to careers involving intercultural communication, diplomacy, or global relations. Religious teachings often provide perspectives on wealth, materialism, and financial stewardship, which can affect career choices. Individuals may consider professions which align with their views on wealth and financial responsibility. Religious beliefs can also shape attitudes toward success and achievement. Some individuals may choose careers that reflect their religious views on the purpose of success and the ethical pursuit of goals.

Education

Religious values may impact decisions regarding education and career training. Some individuals may choose educational paths that align with their religious beliefs or that enable them to pursue careers to attend specific religious institutions (e.g., K-12 schools or certain colleges or universities).

Observance

Religions often emphasize the importance of taking time for spiritual practices. This may influence career choices, with individuals considering professions that allow for periods of personal retreat, meditation, or rest as well as accommodation for religious observances.

Mentorship/Networking

The influence of religious communities and leaders can impact career choices. Guidance, expectations, and networking opportunities from religious authorities or fellow parishioners may shape the career paths individuals choose.

SOCIOECONOMIC STATUS

Socioeconomic status (SES) refers to the relative position of a family or individual within a hierarchical social structure, based on access to or control over wealth, prestige, and power. SES can have a profound impact on an individual's career choices in a number of ways. It is commonly used to measure social class and social status and typically encompasses an individual's or family's social and economic position relative to others in society. SES is often considered a composite measure of income, level of education, and occupational prestige or reputation within the family. It is important to note that while SES can significantly influence career choices, individuals can also demonstrate agency and resilience in navigating their career paths despite, or in spite of, their SES.

Below are several ways in which SES can influence career decisions. Consider the following possibilities and how SES may influence your education and career choices.

Education

Individuals from higher SES backgrounds often have greater access to high quality education, including private schools and extracurricular activities, such as sports teams, music lessons, arts programs, or clubs. These activities provide valuable opportunities for skill development, networking, and personal growth, often giving them an increased competitive advantage in both academic and professional spheres. This access can also influence career choices by providing a foundation that may result in the pursuit of advanced degrees or entering certain professions. People from higher SES backgrounds may have more educational opportunities for enrichment programs, advanced placement courses, and specialized training. These educational advantages can open doors to fields that require specific qualifications. SES can also result in some families having greater financial resources to support further education, including graduate and professional degrees. This financial support can significantly expand the range of available professions.

Individuals from middle and lower SES backgrounds may also have unique educational experiences. Public schools, though often underfunded, can offer strong community engagement and alternative pathways like vocational training, apprenticeships, and scholarships that might open doors to non-traditional or entrepreneurial careers. Despite fewer resources, many people from lower SES backgrounds find ways to excel through perseverance, community networks, and affordable educational options.

Networking

SES can affect the quality and extent of a person's social connections and personal networks. Networking opportunities provided by higher SES networks can significantly influence career choices by offering access to mentorship, job opportunities, and industry insights. Higher SES individuals often have access to successful role models and mentors within their social circles. Exposure to positive career influences can shape career aspirations and choices. Internships and work experience are often critical for career development, and individuals from higher SES backgrounds may have better access to internships, which provide valuable experience that can influence career choices. Furthermore, higher SES individuals may have access to influential professional networks through family connections and prestigious educational institutions, both of which can play a crucial role in career advancement. These individuals are also more likely to have greater access to professional development opportunities, workshops, and conferences, which can enhance skills and open doors to specific career paths. People from lower SES backgrounds may have limited exposure to certain professions and networks, which can influence the range of careers they consider.

While individuals from lower SES backgrounds may experience less access to these exclusive networks, they often can build strong support systems through community organizations, local businesses, and grassroots efforts. These connections can lead to career success in ways that are not always obvious but are no less valuable.

Influence

Higher SES individuals may possess greater cultural capital, which includes the knowledge, skills, and habits valued in certain professions. This cultural capital can facilitate entry into fields that require specific cultural competencies, thereby influencing career choices. SES can shape the types of careers individuals aspire to pursue. For example, individuals from higher SES backgrounds may be more likely to aspire to careers in law, medicine, or finance—fields that often require significant educational and financial investments. Additionally, SES can shape societal expectations and cultural influences regarding suitable career paths. Individuals from higher SES backgrounds can face different societal expectations, which can impact their career trajectories. SES also influences educational choices, such as the decision to attend vocational schools, community colleges, or four-year universities. These choices, in turn, affect the range of career options available to individuals.

Those from middle and lower SES backgrounds may be drawn to careers based on practicality or necessity, such as trades or service industries, but these paths also offer valuable opportunities for success and fulfillment. While SES may influence the level of formal education available, it does not determine personal drive, passion, or the ability to succeed. Individuals from all SES backgrounds can excel through hard work, resilience, and the pursuit of meaningful careers aligned with their strengths and interests.

Security

SES can impact an individual's financial stability and their willingness to take career-related risks. Higher SES individuals may have a financial safety net that allows them to take risks in their careers, such as pursuing entrepreneurship or passion-driven careers. SES can also influence an individual's ability to relocate for career opportunities. Higher SES individuals may have the financial means to move for job prospects, thereby expanding their range of career options. Moreover, SES can influence perceptions of job security and stability. Individuals from lower SES backgrounds may prioritize careers that are perceived as more stable, while those from higher SES backgrounds may have more flexibility to pursue riskier, but potentially more lucrative, opportunities.

Assimilation

SES can influence an individual's perception of workplace culture and fit. Higher SES individuals may prioritize workplaces that align with their values and cultural background, seeking environments where they feel comfortable and supported.

People from lower SES backgrounds also show remarkable adaptability and resilience. Many pursue careers in fields such as healthcare, education, or skilled trades, where job security is paramount, and excel through hard work, determination, and an ability to overcome adversity. These individuals often create their own paths to career

success by leveraging their resourcefulness and work eth-
ic.

TRAUMA

Trauma can have a profound effect on various aspects of
a person's career choices. The effects of trauma are often complex and can depend on the nature, severity, and
timing of the traumatic event(s). It is important to recognize that individuals respond to trauma in diverse ways,
and the impact on career choices is highly individualized.
Professional support, therapy, and a compassionate work
environment can contribute to the healing process and
help individuals make career choices aligned with their
goals and well-being.

Below are several ways in which trauma can influence career decisions. Consider the following possibilities and how
trauma may influence your education and career choices.

Mental & Emotional Health

Trauma can have significant effects on mental and emotional health, leading to conditions such as post-traumat-
ic stress disorder (PTSD), anxiety, or depression. Mental
health challenges may influence an individual's ability to
pursue certain careers or handle specific workplace stres-
sors. Trauma can affect cognitive processes, including decision-making. Individuals who have experienced trauma
may find it challenging to make decisions related to their
careers, such as choosing a path, setting goals, or making
long-term plans.

Trauma can erode self-esteem and confidence, causing individuals to struggle with feelings of inadequacy or

self-doubt. These feelings can impact career choices and limit the willingness to pursue challenging or ambitious paths. Trauma survivors may have difficulty coping with stress, and the demands of certain careers may exacerbate symptoms. As a result, some individuals may choose professions that offer lower stress levels or provide better support for managing stress.

Career choices may also be shaped by how trauma has affected perceptions of self-worth, purpose, and aspirations. Some people may opt for careers that allow for a high degree of control or predictability as a coping strategy. Trauma survivors may prioritize setting boundaries and achieving a healthy work-life balance, seeking stability, predictability, and the ability to maintain a separation between work and personal life. The workplace culture, policies, and organizational support for mental health may play a crucial role in these decisions.

Avoidance/Triggers

Trauma can lead to the development of fears and avoidance behaviors. Individuals may avoid certain career paths, workplaces, or activities that trigger memories or sensations related to the traumatic experience. Certain workplace environments or elements may act as triggers for individuals who have experienced trauma, which can affect their career choices. For example, they may avoid specific industries, work settings, or job responsibilities that evoke traumatic memories.

Trauma survivors may prefer careers that offer a high degree of autonomy and control over their work environment. This can be a way to manage triggers related to perceived loss of control, allowing individuals to mitigate the emotional impact of traumatic reminders in the workplace.

Relationships

Building and maintaining professional relationships can be impacted by the interpersonal challenges associated with trauma. Trust issues, difficulty in forming connections, and fear of vulnerability may hinder networking and collaboration in the workplace. Trauma can also lead to difficulties with authority figures. As a result, some individuals may choose career paths that allow for a more egalitarian or collaborative work environment, minimizing triggers related to authority dynamics and enabling healthier interpersonal interactions.

Education & Advocacy

Trauma can influence decisions related to education and training. Some individuals may find it challenging to engage in formal education or pursue specific training programs due to the emotional and cognitive impact of trauma. Moreover, trauma can lead to shifts in personal interests, values, and priorities. Career choices may reflect these changes as individuals seek professions that align with their evolving sense of purpose and meaning.

Some individuals who have experienced trauma may be drawn to healing professions, such as counseling, therapy, or social work. The desire to help others navigate their own challenges can be a motivating factor in these career choices. Additionally, some individuals may choose careers that allow them to contribute to positive change or use their experiences to help others.

ANYTHING ELSE?

There may be other important factors worth considering. Is there anything else that matters to you? Explore and reflect on anything that is significant to you and your circumstances.

Get to Work

Think about what realizations have you come to about what has shaped you, and your education and career choices. (Use *Career Compass Workbook*, page 6.)

- Which external influences and biases have affected you, and what impact have they had on you?

- What unconscious biases are you now aware of that you hadn't previously considered? How have these biases influenced you?

Check-in

Your story, combined with both your external influences and biases, can shape—and even distort—your interpretation of personal and career identity (answers to "Who am I?" or "What do I want to be?"). Continue to examine and reflect on your current starting point by considering the external factors and variables that have influenced and shaped your thoughts on education and careers. Pay particular attention to areas where you have identified intersections or redundancies. Consider all the factors that have affected you and how they have shaped your beliefs about career choices. Once you complete this exercise,

your mind will be more open to exploring career possibilities, free from biases that could inhibit you.

Chapter Six

Assessment Tools

Assessment tools can be a valuable resource when making career decisions. They can help individuals explore and understand their interests, values, skills, preferences, personality traits, natural abilities, and more. These tools provide insights into strengths and preferences, offering a framework for better understanding personal attributes and inclinations. Career assessments can help clarify career options by identifying important characteristics. They may also present a range of career possibilities that individuals might not have otherwise considered. All these benefits contribute to helping people gain focus and perspective, allowing them to make confident, well-thought-out, and informed decisions about potential career paths.

When reviewing career reports, don't limit yourself to just the careers they list. The suggestions in the reports can often spark ideas for similar careers or lead to new realizations you hadn't considered. By staying open-minded and looking beyond the immediate suggestions, you may discover new possibilities. Let the report be a guide, but remember that your career journey is personal. If a career on the list doesn't interest you, think about what aspects of that work, or work environment, you would enjoy and then explore careers that match those qualities.

There are numerous options available when it comes to taking career assessments. It is important to understand how they work, how they are administered, what they cost, and what information they provide. A career assessment can be called a variety of different things: career test, aptitude test, vocational assessment, etc. Generally speaking, these assessments consist of a series of questions aimed at helping you learn more about yourself so you can discover which jobs align best with your skills, strengths, interests, emotional intelligence, personality, values, goals, and more. Career assessments should be used in conjunction with your own thoughts, ideas, and aspirations. While there is no single assessment tool guaranteed to determine "the perfect career" for you, assessments are a great resource when exploring career options.

It is important to understand the difference between a career assessment and an aptitude test, as the two are often confused. While they share some similarities, they serve different purposes and focus on different aspects of a person's characteristics. Career assessments are designed to help a person explore and evaluate various aspects of their skills, strengths, interests, emotional intelligence, personality, values, goals, and more. In contrast, aptitude tests measure a person's innate or acquired abilities. Aptitude tests are designed to assess a person's potential to perform well in certain types of tasks or roles, such as problem-solving, verbal reasoning, numerical reasoning, spatial reasoning, or mechanical aptitude. Common aptitude tests include the SAT, ACT, MCAT, or LSAT.

Please note that the career assessments reviewed in this chapter do not assess your ability to obtain employment or perform well in specific careers. Instead, they suggest compatibility based on your reported skills, strengths, interests, emotional intelligence, personality, values, goals, etc.

Some career assessments are only available when administered by a qualified professional who can interpret the results. There are also many self-administered career assessments available, some of which are free. Below are several of the more popular, widely used, and easily accessible options for career assessments, each supplemented with a short description of key information and characteristics to consider.

Get Ready to Work!

Below is a list of some of the most widely used career assessment tools. (More information and links are available at vpcareerexploration.com.) Select and complete the career assessment(s) of your choice, and thoroughly review the report(s). Use the lists, information, and suggestions from the assessment results to reflect on your key takeaways. Record your insights in the *Career Compass Workbook* (page 7).

Begin to create a list of career possibilities from your assessment results that you would like to explore further. This list will become your Maybe List, an essential tool to keep yourself organized and intentional during your career exploration process. (Maybe List, *Career Compass Workbook*, page 8.)

MYERS-BRIGGS TYPE INDICATOR

The Myers-Briggs Type Indicator (MBTI) is widely recognized as one of the most effective tools for assessing career preferences and suitability. The MBTI is a personality test that uses your responses to a series of questions to identify one of 16 personality types. The assessment categorizes your preferences in four areas: introversion or extraversion (the source of your energy), sensing or intuition (how you take in information), thinking or feeling (how you make decisions), and judging or perceiving (how you deal with the world). Understanding your personality type can provide valuable insights, including identifying careers that complement your personality preferences. It can also help guide you in exploring career options that align with your personality, specifically by identifying communication styles, team dynamics, strengths, weaknesses, conflict resolution, decision-making, leadership style, the effects of stress, learning and work preferences.

The official MBTI® Career Assessment is only available if administered by a qualified practitioner or via mbtionl ine.com. Unofficial versions that use similar methods and principles are also available online. Some charge a fee to take the assessment, while a free version is available at 16personalities.com.

STRONG INTEREST INVENTORY

The Strong Interest Inventory® (SII) is a popular assessment used to identify career interests, also referred to as "work personality." The tool uses Six Occupational Themes (derived from the Holland Code) as its benchmark and compares your interests to those of others who are satisfied with their career choices. The Six Occupational Themes are: Realistic, Investigative, Artistic, Social, Enterprising, and Conventional (RIASEC). The basic premise of the SII is that a person's personal interests correlate with occupational preferences. After completing the assessment, up to three of your highest occupational themes are identified.

The report then provides lists of occupation possibilities based on your interests.

The official SII® offers several versions designed for high school students, college students, and adults. The official Strong Interest Inventory can only be administered by a qualified practitioner, although there are self-administered versions available online, many of which require payment.

Author's Note

Many other career assessment tools use the Holland Code/Six Occupational Themes/RIASEC model (several others are covered below). For example, the Xello assessment (help.xello.world) also uses this model and is commonly administered to public high school students.

MY NEXT MOVE

My Next Move (mynextmove.org) uses the O*NET Interest Profiler to assess your work interests. This free assessment is similar to the SII but is shorter and does not generate a customized report. It identifies your top three interests and then allows you to select one of five "Job Zones" based on the level of experience, education, and training you have or are interested in pursuing. The results are linked to a list of careers that match your interest and preparation level, marked as "Best Fit" or "Great Fit." This site provides a one page snap-shot career summary for career matches, which includes a 60–90 second video explanations/summary. (A supplemental and more in-depth career report is available at onetonline.org.)

SELF-DIRECTED SEARCH TEST

The Self-Directed Search (SDS) test uses the same career theory principles as the Strong Interest Inventory and My Next Move. It evaluates six occupational themes (RIASEC) and matches the results with jobs based on competencies, aspirations, interests, and activities. The report provides a personalized summary with best-fitting career options, salary information, and educational opportunities. Special reports are available for older job seekers and students. The assessment can be purchased at <u>self-directed-search.co</u> <u>m</u>.

ENNEAGRAM OF PERSONALITY

The Enneagram of Personality uses nine distinct and interrelated personality types to enhance self-awareness and inform career decisions. These types include: Reformer, Helper, Achiever, Individualist, Investigator, Loyalist, Enthusiast, Challenger, and Peacemaker. The Enneagram Type Report offers insights into core motivations, preferences, stress, fears, desires, growth, and development. Rather than focusing only on skills, interests, and values, the Enneagram combines these insights to help understand a person's multifaceted personality and how it correlates with career-related attributes.

The official Enneagram assessment can be taken for a fee at <u>enneagraminstitute.com</u>. Several unofficial versions are available online, some offering free initial tests, but charging for detailed reports.

KEIRSEY TEMPERAMENT SORTER

This personality assessment categorizes your personality into one of four basic types: Idealist, Rational, Guardian, or Artisan. The assessment aims to help you understand your motivations and decision-making style, which can be helpful when exploring career options. After completing the test, you will receive a report outlining your personality type and corresponding career options. The assessment is free at keirsey.com, though there may be a fee to access the full report.

SIGI 3

The System of Interactive Guidance and Information (SIGI 3) assesses your values, skills, personality traits, and interests to generate a list of potential careers. A unique feature of SIGI 3 is its detailed career information, including job descriptions, educational requirements, salary expectations, and job outlook. SIGI 3 is often free for students through many colleges and universities. Individuals can also purchase a 90-day access pass at sigi3.org.

MYPLAN

MyPlan.com offers a free assessment that identifies your values and provides insights into motivations and career needs. Specific resources are available for students in middle school, high school, and college, as well as for adults in career transition. The report suggests 739 job options that may fit your specific needs. Additional paid assessments include a career personality test, career interest inventory, and career skills profiler.

CAREERFITTER

CareerFitter.com offers a free assessment that identifies your work personality. The results help identify which job environments, careers, and tasks align with your personality (categorized as quest, style, and strength). A premium version of the assessment is available for a fee and includes additional career matching and hundreds of career reports.

RASMUSSEN UNIVERSITY

Rasmussen University (rasmussen.edu) provides a free career assessment that uses skills matches to suggest multiple career options. The assessment takes into account seven categories: artistic, interpersonal, communication, managerial, mathematics, mechanical, and science. Results can be filtered by job growth and education level, though suggested careers may align with Rasmussen University's educational programs.

Author's Note

Rasmussen University is just one example of a school that offers career assessments for potential students. Research other nearby or online schools to see if they have skill/interest match assessments.

One thing to be aware of when using career assessment tools linked to a specific school is that the assessment results are likely limited to matching programs available at that school.

MAPP TEST

The Motivational Appraisal of Personal Potential (MAPP) test identifies your motivations, preferences, work habits, and strengths in relation to career options. The test includes insights into how you interact socially at work, approach tasks, and collaborate with others. The basic assessment is free, with a paid option for a more detailed report. The MAPP assessment is available at <u>assessment</u> <u>.com</u>.

SOKANU CAREER TEST

The Sokanu assessment helps you find careers that match your personality traits by analyzing five factors: personality archetype, history, interests, career goals, and work environment. The assessment is free at <u>careerexplorer.com</u> and includes career and degree matches.

PREDICTIVE INDEX BEHAVIORAL ASSESSMENT

This assessment uses personality traits to predict how you'll perform in various work environments. It assesses behavioral drives, needs, conflict, stress, leadership, and teamwork styles. The test is free at <u>predictiveindex.com</u>.

CLIFTON STRENGTHS

Clifton Strengths is not a career assessment tool and it will not tell you which careers your strengths are well suited for. Clifton Strengths is a tool from positive psychology designed to identify and help you develop your natural talents into strengths. It identifies your top five strengths (or more, with an advanced purchase). The assessment helps you understand how to apply your strengths in school and work to increase productivity, engagement, and happiness. The book StrengthsFinder 2.0 from Gallup includes an access code to complete the assessment.

Get to Work

Select and complete a career assessment(s), then review their report(s). Use the reports suggestions to begin considering potential careers. What other career options come to mind that are not included in the assessment reports? (Use the *Career Compass Workbook*, pages 7–8).

- What have you learned about yourself from the assessment(s) in terms of your personality, interest, values, strengths, etc.?

- What personal characteristics are important for you to consider when exploring different career paths?

- Begin compiling career ideas on your Maybe List.

Check-in

Career assessments are valuable tools for self-reflection and career exploration, but they should never be viewed as the sole determinant of your career path. Some individuals place too much weight on the results, allowing them to dictate their choices without considering other factors. Others may dismiss them entirely, missing out on insights that could help guide their journey. Career assessments can be extremely useful as a starting point in the career exploration process. They provide valuable information to help you understand and articulate your skills, strengths, interests, emotional intelligence, personality, values, goals, and more. However, it is important to supplement these results with personal experiences and additional research—which is coming next!

Part 1: Recap
Understand Yourself

Congratulations on taking the time and putting in the effort to understand who you are before making a decision about what you want to be! You have worked to understand your story up until this point in your life and the various unique factors that have shaped your personal identity. This self-awareness will enable you to make informed and thoughtful career choices.

To recap, you should now have a list of things you are good at, activities you enjoy, a list of your core values, and ideas for how you envision your future.

In addition, you have worked to identify any external factors and biases that have (consciously or unconsciously) influenced or distorted your thoughts and ideas about career choices. These external influences and biases may include, but are not limited to, culture, disability, gender, gender identity and sexual orientation, parents, peers, religion, trauma, or anything else that you've realized plays a role in shaping your perspective. With this awareness and understanding, clarity can be achieved as you move forward to evaluate what career industries and professions might be well-suited for you.

Finally, you have taken the time to select and complete one or more career assessments to understand your personal skills, strengths, interests, emotional intelligence, personality, values, goals, and more. These assessments can help you gain clarity and identify important characteristics to consider when exploring different career paths. Depending on the assessments you selected, you should now have some new ideas about careers that are suggested as potential "matches" for you. You should have also begun a Maybe List of career options based on the assessment results.

Be sure to add any other career ideas you have to your Maybe List, even if they weren't included in your assessment results. This list will evolve, expand, and narrow as you continue to explore. Adding a career to your Maybe List is not a commitment—it is simply a note to yourself that this is a career you may want to learn more about and consider.

Having now completed all of this work to better understand yourself, you are now ready to move on to the next step in the process: Additional Considerations.

Part 2 - Additional Considerations

Author's Note

For the sake of simplicity and consistency, I use certain generic terms repeatedly throughout this book (and the *Career Compass Workbook*). Please keep in mind that, at times, these terms may not fully reflect your specific situation. Feel free to mentally substitute the term that best applies to you.

College: All post-secondary school options, since they all serve as pathways to further education or career development after high school.

College Student: All post-secondary students, regardless of age or the type of post-secondary option.

Degree: Any certification, training, credential, associate degree, bachelor's degree, master's degree, or other academic qualification.

Chapter Seven

Preparation

With the right information, inspiration can follow. Before you decide to pursue a career, you should have a plan on how to successfully achieve your career objective. Taking simple steps during your preparation can help you effectively explore your career options and position yourself for successful implementation.

Thoughtfully consider how the information presented in this chapter can help you prepare to make informed career decisions—and then implement them. Equip yourself with the knowledge and understanding of how the topics—research, finances, career tools, and networking—apply to you.

Get Ready to Work!

Consider how the following topics can help you gain clarity and a solid understanding to make informed decisions during your career exploration and planning process. (*Career Compass Workbook*, page 10).

RESEARCH

Below are resources to help you conduct thoughtful and thorough career research. These resources include national sources, educational institutions, military services, informational websites, local resources, labor market and potential earnings, and potential employers.

National Resources

Many national resources available to assist in career exploration. The following national resources provide valuable information, tools, and support when researching occupations, searching for job openings, or seeking career advice.

My Next Move (mynextmove.org) is an excellent and free resource for conducting preliminary career research. It contains a comprehensive database of occupational information maintained by the U.S. Department of Labor, covering over 1,000 occupations. Below are some of the features of this website:

- A quick search on the main page using "Search careers with keywords" will produce a list of closely matched jobs. When a career is selected, a job summary report appears, highlighting the knowledge, skills, abilities, personality traits, technology, education, and outlook for that career. The report is brief, easy to read, and organized in a way that makes key information easily accessible. With just a few additional clicks, you can explore more detailed information, especially in the Education and Job Outlook categories.

- Another search option on the main page is "Browse careers by industry." Over 20 industries are listed, and each one produces an extensive list of the types of careers within that industry. The same job summary reports are available for each career on the list with just a click.

- Yellow suns mark specific jobs with a "bright outlook," indicating careers expected to experience rapid growth in the coming years.

- On the job summary page for most careers, there is also a 60–90 second video featuring key information about the career. These videos provide valuable insights and visual examples of the career in action, offering a quick preview of what the career entails.

Onetonline.org (O*Net) is similar to My Next Move as it contains a comprehensive database of occupational information maintained by the U.S. Department of Labor for over 1,000 occupations and provides several advanced search features to assist in career exploration. O*Net has all the same occupations in its database as My Next Move and offers the same Occupation Keyword Search feature, which produces a list of closely matched careers, listed in order by the closest match. It also has additional search tools, including Find Occupations, Advanced Search, O*Net Data, and Crosswalk.

The career reports on O*Net are more detailed and lengthy than those on My Next Move. These reports include comprehensive descriptions of occupations, including required skills, abilities, work activities, and career pathways, making O*Net ideal for transitioning to in-depth career research. Below are some of the features of this website and its advanced search options and reports:

- Occupation-Specific Information (with detailed lists of tasks and technology skills)

- Occupational Requirements (with detailed lists of work activities, detailed work activities, and work context)

- Experience Requirements (with detailed lists of job zone, apprenticeship opportunities, and training & credentials, including search engine features for state and local training and certifications)

- Worker Requirements (with detailed lists of skills, knowledge, and education)

- Worker Characteristics (with detailed lists of abilities, interests—including the assigned occupational theme(s), work values, and work styles)

- Workforce Characteristics (with search engine features for wages, employment trends, and job openings on the web)

- More Information (with lists and links to related occupations and sources of additional information)

The Find Occupations feature offers several methods to narrow your search criteria, including Bright Outlook, Career Cluster, Hot Technology, Industry, Job Family, Job Zone, STEM, and All Occupations. Each category offers more specific subcategories (for example, in "Bright Outlook", you can specifically search for Rapid Growth, Numerous Job Openings, New and Emerging, and All Bright Outlook Jobs). Selections result in a list of occupations, which are then linked to career reports.

The Advanced Search feature offers several methods to narrow your search criteria, including Job Duties, Professional Associations, Related Activities, Soft Skills, and

Technology Skills. Each category offers even more specific subcategories or search engine features.

The O*Net Data feature offers several methods to narrow your search criteria, including Abilities, Interests, Knowledge, Skills (Basic), Skills (Cross-Functional), Work Activities, Work Context, Work Styles, and Work Values. Each category offers even more specific subcategories or search features. One of the more useful search features is under Interest, where you can use Occupational Theme(s) to correlate interests to career matches. Occupational themes align with the RIASEC model (also known as the Holland Codes, discussed in Chapter 6 under STRONG INTEREST INVENTORY) to assist individuals in career exploration. By navigating to the O*Net Data section and selecting the Interests subsection, you can use the "Browse by Interest" page to discover occupation ideas that align with a single or combination of interest areas.

Browse by Interests

Interests are preferences for work environments and outcomes. Select an interest to discover occupations that support the interest area.

Want to discover your interests? Take the O*NET Interest Profiler at My Next Move.

Realistic
Work involves designing, building, or repairing of equipment, materials, or structures, engaging in physical activity or working outdoors. Realistic occupations are often associated with engineering, mechanics and electronics, construction, woodworking, transportation, machine operation, agriculture, animal services, physical or manual labor, athletics, or protective services.

Investigative
Work involves studying and researching non-living objects, living organisms, disease or other forms of impairment, or human behavior. Investigative occupations are often associated with physical, life, medical, or social sciences, and can be found in the fields of humanities, mathematics/statistics, information technology, or health care service.

Artistic
Work involves creating original visual artwork, performances, written works, food, or music for a variety of media, or applying artistic principles to the design of various objects and materials. Artistic occupations are often associated with visual arts, applied arts and design, performing arts, music, creative writing, media, or culinary art.

Social
Work involves helping, teaching, advising, assisting, or providing service to others. Social occupations are often associated with social, health care, personal service, teaching/education, or religious activities.

Enterprising
Work involves managing, negotiating, marketing, or selling, typically in a business setting, or leading or advising people in political and legal situations. Enterprising occupations are often associated with business initiatives, sales, marketing/advertising, finance, management/administration, professional advising, public speaking, politics, or law.

Conventional
Work involves following procedures and regulations to organize information or data, typically in a business setting. Conventional occupations are often associated with office work, accounting, mathematics/statistics, information technology, finance, or human resources.

The Interest feature can be used in different ways on O*Net. While on a specific careers report, under the Work Characteristics section, specifically within the Interests subsection, each career is assigned an Interest Code. This code corresponds to the RIASEC/Holland Code, helping users better understand how different careers align with their interests and personality traits based on the model.

Browse by Interests

Have a three-letter interest code? You can focus your search by choosing up to three interest areas, to see the occupations which match your choices.

First Interest   Second Interest   Third Interest
R — Realistic   ∨   None   ∨   None   ∨   Go

Want to discover your interests? Take the O*NET Interest Profiler at My Next Move.

NCDA (National Career Development Association at nc da.org) is a professional organization that promotes career development and provides resources for individuals seeking career guidance. Their website offers articles, webinars, and resources on career development and exploration.

BLS (Bureau of Labor Statistics at bls.gov) provides extensive information on various occupations, including job duties, educational requirements, median pay, and job outlook. The BLS maintains the Occupational Outlook Handbook, which can be used in conjunction with O*Net's Crosswalk feature.

DOL (U.S. Department of Labor at dol.gov), through the ETA (Employment and Training Administration), offers a wide range of resources and programs to assist individuals with career exploration. The DOL/ETA supports training, education, and employment, including One-Stop Career Centers, apprenticeships, programs, and workforce development initiatives.

U.S. Census Bureau (census.gov) provides valuable insights into labor market trends, industry dynamics, occupational characteristics, educational opportunities, geographic considerations, and economic conditions. The Census Bureau collects and publishes data on the labor market, employment trends, unemployment rates, wages, occupations, industries, and workforce demographics. Understanding this data can help raise awareness of the labor market and identify potential career opportunities.

Educational Institutions

High schools and colleges play a crucial role in helping students explore career options and make informed decisions about their future. Educational institutions can provide many resources available to current and future students to assist with career exploration. (A quick word of caution: when utilizing the resources available through colleges, be aware that the options presented may be limited based on the fields of study offered.)

Thoroughly and thoughtfully research the different educational pathways for the careers you are interested in pursuing. These pathways may include various certification, training, credential, Associate Degree, Bachelor's Degree, Master's Degree, etc.

Other options for researching college opportunities include talking to mentors, networking (including professional associations, which are also listed on O*Net under "More Information"), and conducting additional internet research. For example, try searching "What are the schools for [career] in the [location] area?" to find valuable information.

After identifying the degree required for your chosen career, compile a list of possible schools. Next, research each option in more detail. When doing so, carefully consider factors such as admission requirements, the education timeline, and associated costs and fees. Determine how long it will take to obtain the necessary education and training for that career.

On-the-job training is provided by some employers who do not require formal education or training. Apprenticeship programs may be an attractive option, as they provide income during training and guarantee employment after successful completion. Research which industries and companies offer these opportunities, and think about how you can position yourself to stand out in the application and hiring process.

Career counseling services are provided by staff who can offer personalized guidance and support to students at most schools. The counseling services can assist students in assessing their interests, strengths, and goals, and in exploring potential career paths that align with their aspirations. Many will offer assessment tools and resources to help students gain insights into their skills, preferences, and potential career matches (Chapter 6). Career resource centers are typically equipped with information, resources, and tools to support students in their career exploration and job search. Colleges and universities should provide information in pamphlet form at the resource center or on their website, detailing career options for specific majors or fields of study offered at that institution. These resources can be incredibly helpful, especially when creating Career Plans and Action Plans (Chapter 14), as they often outline detailed education plans for completing degree requirements.

Career workshops, or career events, provide students with an informational environment to explore various career-related topics. These events or activities may include career fairs, networking events (with professionals to conduct informational interviews), career tools workshops (resume writing, job search strategies, interview preparation), or lectures on industry trends. Schools often have partnerships with industry organizations, companies, and professionals, and will host guest speakers at campus events, providing firsthand knowledge and perspectives on different career paths and industries. These events offer valuable insights and practical advice for students as they explore career options.

Internships allow for students to work with companies that provide hands-on, real-life experiences in fields of interest. Internships can offer exposure to different industries, roles, and work environments, helping students make informed and educated career decisions.

Many schools often have established alumni networks that offer mentorship programs, allowing current students to connect with alumni working in areas of interest. These networks provide opportunities for informational interviews or job shadowing, offering insights, advice, and practical opportunities to help students better understand and navigate their career paths. The alumni network often continues to provide support even after graduation.

Faculty advisors at schools provide guidance and support to students on academics and careers. Students may be able to schedule personal appointments to discuss their career interests, goals, and concerns, and receive advice and support.

Career development workshops or classes are available at many schools, some as a credit course. These classes can focus on general career exploration for students who are undecided about their career path or college major. They can also be part of the curriculum for a specific field of study, taken before declaring a major, to ensure thorough exploration and awareness of the possible careers in that area (such as Careers in Psychology).

Military Service

Joining a branch of the military can be a valuable option for individuals considering a structured career path. Different branches of the military offer a range of entry points depending on your age and qualifications. The military also administers its own aptitude and career assessments to help you identify roles that align with your skills and interests within their structure. Upon joining, you'll receive job-specific training, which can set you up with valuable experience in a wide range of fields. In addition to career development, military service can be a gateway to financial assistance for further education and training once your service is completed. Many resources are available to explore this option and understand how it can support your career interests. USA.gov's military service page is a great place to begin exploring these career options (usa.gov/military-and-veterans).

Each different military branch has their own unique characteristics, but they all share some similarities. Each branch's websites offer detailed information on recruitment, career options, training programs, and financial benefits like education assistance. Connecting with local recruiters is typically easy, and recruiters can provide you with specific insights into the opportunities available in each branch.

- Army: goarmy.com

- Navy: navy.mil

- Air Force: airforce.com

- Marine Corps: marines.com

- Space Force: spaceforce.com

- National Guard (US National Guard): nationalguard.com

- State National Guard: nationalguard.com/select-your-state

Informational Websites

Numerous informational websites that can help people explore job opportunities and industries. It can be difficult to know which ones to use and when. While My Next Move and O*Net have already been discussed, there are more websites that can be used in your career research.

Company review sites can show employee ratings, salary information, job functions, insights into company leadership, work environment, and corporate culture. These reviews can provide valuable information during career exploration, helping you assess compatibility with potential employers. Some of the company review websites include Glassdoor, Vault, and CareerBliss.

Job search engines, like Monster, CareerBuilder, or Indeed, allow users to search for current job openings based on keywords and locations. Using job search engines in career research can provide valuable information regarding job titles, availability, salary, and required skills, experience, and education.

USAJOBS.gov is the official job site of the United States federal government. It posts federal job openings, provides information on career paths within the federal government, and outlines the application process for government jobs.

LinkedIn is the leading professional networking platform and can be a valuable tool for career exploration, professional networking, job searching, and personal branding. LinkedIn advertises job openings, connects users with professionals in their fields of interest, and hosts industry groups.

Business journals provide valuable information, insights, and resources for individuals exploring career opportunities. Business journals feature articles, market research, and reports on industry trends, developments, and emerging opportunities. Geographically specific business journals may report on local job openings, hiring trends, and growing companies and industries.

Local Resources

Utilizing local resources can also provide valuable information for people exploring careers. Become aware of which resources are available in your area and how to best utilize them.

Every city, county, and state is unique, making it impossible to include a comprehensive list of all the recommended resources to investigate. The following suggestions may or may not exist in your area, and it is highly likely that there are additional resources available that are not listed here. Be vigilant and thorough in your research to identify local resources that can assist with your career exploration.

Chamber of Commerce groups can offer resources and programs to support local businesses and job seekers in your community. The Chamber of Commerce can help people explore and connect with local employers by hosting networking events, job fairs, and collaborating with startup companies in the area.

Public libraries provide free access to books, magazines, and online resources. Libraries often offer resources and programs to assist with career exploration and development. Some public libraries even provide career services such as job search skills, interview preparation, and assistance with writing resumes and cover letters.

One Stop Career Centers (also called "One-Stop Shops") offer a range of career resources and services in-person in cities throughout the U.S. These services may include career counseling, job search assistance, workshops, and access to local job listings. Many of these services are also available virtually for added convenience and accessibility. Additionally, these centers are often aware of local job training programs and workforce development initiatives.

Networking events and groups host meetups in the community, providing opportunities to connect with professionals, learn about different industries, and explore career options. Meetup.com, Facebook groups, and your local Chamber of Commerce are great resources for locating these types of events and groups.

Nonprofit organizations and community-based agencies may offer career development programs and services tailored to the needs of specific populations, such as youth, veterans, or people with disabilities.

LABOR MARKET & POTENTIAL EARNINGS

O*Net uses data from the U.S. Department of Labor to provide valuable information and insights on the labor market and potential earnings. Being informed on these topics can help you identify careers that have a positive employment outlook and salaries that correspond with your future life goals. O*Net provides statistics on Median, State, and Local Wages; Employment; Projected Growth; Projected Job Openings; and State Trends. This data can provide a clearer understanding of the labor market, helping you make informed decisions about career opportunities and future prospects. In addition, the interactive tools for State and Local Wages can be especially informative to understand annual and hourly wages ranges according to location.

To continue your research use O*Net and/or job search engines to find current job postings in areas where you would consider living. Consider the following questions:

- How many job postings are available?

- What education, experience, and skills are required for qualified candidates?

- What companies are hiring?

- What is the advertised salary?

You may also want to consider the global perspective of the career field. In today's interconnected world, having a global mindset and understanding international trends can be advantageous. Also, understand how technological advancements and innovations may affect specific career fields. Embracing technology and being tech-savvy can enhance competitiveness in the labor market. This research can be done through a variety of means, depending on what information and field you are researching. Some options include:

- Academic databases including research papers, articles, and journals

- Industry reports, such as McKinsey & Company, Deloitte Insights, PWC, and KPMG

- International organizations and think tanks, such as the World Economic Forum, United Nations, International Labor Organization, and Organization for Economic Co-operation and Development

- Global business news outlets, such as The Financial Times, The Economist, Harvard Business Review, TechCrunch, and Wired

- Professional associations (career field specific)

- Online social media associations, such as LinkedIn

- Online forums, such as Glassdoor

Potential Employers

Research potential employers. The labor market research can be used to identify potential employers in a career field. Use your research to identify companies that are currently hiring and then research those companies. Additional resources that may be helpful are websites like Glassdoor and LinkedIn. Consider the following questions:

- What do current and former employees say about the job, work environment, company culture?

- What kind of training/education, experience and skills do they specify on their job postings?

- How competitive is it to secure a position with this company and in this field? What are your chances of being hired, and what steps can you take to improve your chances and gain a competitive edge?

- Would you want to work for these companies? (Your answer may factor in company culture, work location, salary, benefits, promotion opportunities, etc.)

FINANCES

Understanding money and its role in your career and life is more complex than just salary figures. In addition to researching potential earnings, other important financial factors can help you navigate your career exploration and make informed decisions. After all, the time we spend at work is done in exchange for monetary compensation.

Your financial considerations will likely extend beyond the potential paycheck, but they should also factor into your degree decisions and how you can achieve your financial goals. Gaining a clear understanding of these financial variables is crucial to making choices that help you gain clarity during your career planning and set you up for future success.

Financial Literacy

Being financially literate can be incredibly helpful as you plan and navigate your career journey. With a strong financial education, you'll be able to evaluate how the career decisions you make can impact your income, savings, and expenses. You will also know how to create a budget to effectively manage your finances. Several ways are available to learn financial literacy, including:

- Taking online classes or enrolling in courses at a community college or adult education center.

- Reading books or articles on personal finance.

- Listening to or watching money-themed podcasts or YouTube channels.

- Attending workshops or seminars.

- Asking for guidance from a trusted family member or friend.

Being financially literate allows you to carefully analyze the costs versus the potential benefits before committing to any educational or training program. You will be able to consider not only the tuition and fees associated with the degree program but also additional expenses such as books, materials, transportation, and living costs. Further-

more, you'll be equipped to evaluate your long-term return on investment (ROI)—how the degree will impact your
career prospects and potential earnings, both immediately
and in the future.

Cost of Living

Cost of living is important to consider when exploring career choices. In addition to researching potential earnings
in different careers and industries, it is crucial to determine
whether those earnings will support the actual cost of
living based on your particular circumstances.

A great resource to learn about and estimate cost of
living is by using the MIT Living Wage Calculator (living
wage.mit.edu). This tool is designed and intended to "help
individuals, communities, employers, and others estimate
the local wage rate that a full-time worker requires to cover
the costs of their family's basic needs where they live." You
begin by selecting a State, then County. The results provide
data for 12 different family circumstances giving a comprehensive view of what is needed to financially maintain
various standards of living.

Paying for School/Training

The cost of a degree can be a significant barrier for many
people when considering different career options. While
some people use savings or receive family support, many
other people require financial assistance to be able to af-
ford the degree needed to pursue certain career paths.
High tuition fees and the expense of college can make certain careers seem out of reach. It is important to research
and understand the various ways to fund or finance your
degree, which can unlock opportunities that you might

otherwise overlook or dismiss. Several financial options can help make college more accessible.

Financial Aid

Financial aid is money that helps you pay for school. It is typically offered through colleges. The funding sources include the federal government, state governments, colleges, and private organizations. The most common types of financial aid include grants, scholarships, work-study opportunities, and student loans. To be eligible for financial aid, you must complete the Free Application for Federal Student Aid (FAFSA). Upon completion, your FAFSA Submission Summary (FSS), also known as the Student Aid Report (SAR), a document summarizing your financial aid eligibility, is sent to up to 20 colleges that you request. This allows the college to determine your eligibility for different types of assistance. It is important to pay close attention to application openings and deadlines, as funds are often limited and are awarded on a first-come, first-served basis and may have specific deadlines.

The college will then put together a financial aid offer, or "award." You are not required to accept the entirety of a financial aid offer. Carefully review and consider all options available to you. Be mindful of any terms and conditions that apply to each form of financial assistance.

Student loans are a common component of financial aid and they require careful consideration. Student loans allow you to borrow money for tuition and other expenses, with repayment typically starting shortly after graduation. Student loans can come from several sources, each with its own terms and conditions. The most common types are federal (government) loans, private loans, and school-based loans. Each loan type can have different interest rates, repayment plans, and borrower protections, so it is vital to fully understand the financial commitment before accepting them.

If you consider taking out loans to cover these costs, it is important to assess how much debt you will incur over the time of your degree(s) and whether your future income will be sufficient to manage loan repayments without financial strain. By taking the time to weigh both the financial investment and the potential career outcomes, you can make a more informed decision about whether the degree is worth the cost.

In addition to scholarships offered through financial aid, you should also pursue outside scholarships that you may qualify for. Use career guidance offices, online scholarship search engines, and explore community organizations, businesses, and industry-specific or niche scholarships.

Lastly, research whether your state sponsors any free job training and education programs that could help you gain the necessary skills without incurring (significant) costs.

CAREER TOOLS

Career tools is a term to describe the skill set needed to effectively navigate the job application and hiring process, such as completing online applications, constructing an effective resume and cover letters, knowing how to utilize your personal and professional network, and perfecting your interviewing skills.

Prepare yourself with the knowledge of how to efficiently and effectively use career tools to your advantage to help you achieve your professional goals. It is your responsibility to understand how to successfully use career tools throughout your professional lifetime. Skills, training, and education are not always enough to secure the position you desire.

Author's Note

This book is not about how to get or use career tools. Possessing and knowing how to use career tools is essential to navigating the labor market and obtaining employment. It is important to acknowledge that navigating the labor market can be challenging. Securing a job can be difficult, even with the right training, education, experience, and skills. Professional networking, finding and applying for jobs, customizing cover letters and resumes, and nailing interviews is hard work that can take a significant emotional and psychological toll. Throughout the remainder of this book, I will revisit the topic of career tools multiple times. This is necessary, as I want to remind you to take advantage of opportunities to build and refine your career tools, giving yourself the best possible advantages when it is time to navigate the labor market.

If you are interested, there are additional resources available at vpcareerexploration.com on how to get and use career tools in a downloadable free document, Career Services Resource Guide.

NETWORKING

Building and nurturing a strong personal and professional network is essential for the success of your future career.

The idea of networking can often have a negative connotation, as if it involves using personal relationships solely for professional gain. This perspective can make networking feel superficial or disingenuous. However, think about the idea of networking to make it more approachable and meaningful.

Everyone has a personal network. This includes family, friends, teachers, coaches, and any community you are part of—whether it is a club, a church, or a volunteer organization. These are people who care about you and want the best for you. If they are able to help you, they do so willingly because they value your well-being and success.

In addition to your personal network, you will eventually have—or you already have—a professional network. This network includes co-workers, bosses, supervisors, clients, customers, contractors, and anyone else you interact with professionally. Building this network is important, as these relationships can offer unique opportunities and guidance as you advance in your career.

Networking is not about asking for jobs, but rather about seeking advice, insights, and direction from others. Most people are more than willing to offer guidance and share their knowledge with individuals who they care about or respect. Networking is not a one-sided transaction—it is about fostering give-and-take relationships. Sometimes, you will be the recipient of support, and other times, you will have the opportunity to offer help in return. The key is mutual respect and reciprocity.

Use the *Career Compass Workbook* to map out your network (page 11). You might be surprised at how many people you know who would be eager to support your career if you simply reached out and asked. The types of help you may receive from your personal and professional network can include valuable knowledge, industry insights, emotional support, practical advice, and even career opportunities.

As you prepare for your future career, it is essential to build a reputation for hard work, reliability, and integrity within your network. When interacting with friends, family, classmates, teachers, supervisors, or co-workers, you are already establishing your professional reputation. Remember, your network will be more inclined to help you in the future if you've built a reputation as someone who is dependable, respectful, and committed. The relationships you cultivate today can play a key role in opening doors to you professionally tomorrow.

As you move forward in your career, you will see how critical networking can be when it comes to finding employment. The majority of job opportunities are filled due to personal relationships and networking. Your network is key to navigating the "hidden labor market," as most job openings are never publicly advertised. Some estimates suggest that as much as 70–80% of positions are filled without an open job listing. When hiring, most companies prefer personal referrals over candidates who only apply online. Additionally, many companies prioritize hiring from within or look to candidates who have participated in internships or trainee programs, as these individuals are already familiar with the company culture and have demonstrated their skills and commitment.

Below are additional strategies to help you to prepare to cultivate and build your network.

Networking Events

Consider joining professional networking groups in your area. Professional networking groups often meet once or twice a month for meals or social gatherings to provide opportunities for members to connect, share industry insights, and exchange advice. These events can be an excellent way to build relationships with others, stay informed about trends and opportunities, and even find potential mentors or collaborators. Being active in these groups can expand your network, enhance your career prospects, and provide valuable support as you navigate your professional journey.

Organizations like Chambers of Commerce and Rotary Clubs are excellent and accessible starting points to building meaningful professional connections. These organizations bring together local business leaders, entrepreneurs, and community members and offer regular opportunities for networking. By attending meetings or events, you can connect with local professionals and potentially find new clients, partners, or mentors.

Industry-specific events, conferences, and industry-related gatherings can also provide valuable opportunities to meet professionals in your field, exchange ideas, and build meaningful connections. These events allow you to stay updated on the latest industry trends, emerging technologies, and best practices, helping you remain competitive and informed. They also offer a chance to engage with thought leaders, expand your knowledge, and even potentially discover new career opportunities. Whether through workshops, panel discussions, or casual networking sessions, attending these events can be a powerful way to grow your professional network and enhance your career prospects.

Online Networking

LinkedIn is the leading online platform for professional networking. It provides numerous opportunities for research, as well to build and enhance your career.

Start by creating a strong, detailed profile that highlights your skills, experience, and accomplishments. Make sure to consistently update your profile to reflect your most recent achievements and career developments. Engage with your network by connecting with contacts, and actively give and request endorsements. These actions help strengthen your professional presence and credibility, making you more visible to potential employers, collaborators, and mentors.

Mentorship

Seek mentorship from experienced professionals in your field. A mentor can offer valuable guidance, share industry insights, and help you navigate challenges that arise in your career. By learning from their experiences and expertise, you can gain a clearer perspective on your professional goals, avoid common pitfalls, and make more informed decisions. Mentorship can also provide emotional support, encouragement, and accountability, helping you stay focused and motivated as you progress in your career.

Get to Work

Think about ways you can prepare yourself now, to set yourself up for success throughout your career journey. Decide which resource(s) you will use to conduct preliminary research into what careers you are interested in. While continuing to compile your list of career possibilities, are there any other options that you could add to, or take off, the Maybe List?

- What resources were most helpful in your research?

- Reflect on your financial goals and create a budget to assess how your education or training choices will align with your career and financial goals.

- Identify which career tools you have and need to ensure you are in a good position to navigate the job application and hiring process. Make a plan to get the career tools you lack.

- Use the *Career Compass Workbook* to create a map of your network (page 11).

Check-in

Prepare yourself for success at every stage of your journey by taking proactive steps in your career preparation. Learn how to research potential career options and gather information about labor markets, potential earnings, and educational pathways using resources like O*Net. Consider your financial situation, including the cost of living, education and training expenses, and the return on your financial investment. Think about your network and how building personal and professional connections can unlock opportunities and foster career growth. The better you prepare in these areas, the more opportunities you'll uncover, increasing your chances of finding career paths that are a good fit for you.

Chapter Eight

Mindset

During the career exploration process, your mindset plays a crucial role in shaping your decisions. It is important to stay open, flexible, and adaptable. Understand that your career path may change after you make a decision—and that's completely normal! Be willing to adjust your plans as new opportunities come your way. Trust your instincts, but remember that no career is without its challenges. Don't let setbacks discourage you; perseverance is key to achieving anything worthwhile, including the career and future you want.

Resilience means bouncing back stronger after each challenge, understanding that every setback is an opportunity for growth. It involves being kind to yourself when things don't go as planned, and maintaining the courage to keep pushing forward despite the obstacles. Resilience is what transforms failure into learning and transforms uncertainty into progress. The more you develop and practice resilience, the more equipped you will be to navigate the ups and downs of your career journey, ultimately helping you achieve success.

Get Ready to Work!

Consider the following possibilities and how they might positively (or negatively) impact your mindset during your career exploration and professional journey. Use the *Career Compass Workbook* to record your thoughts and ideas (page 12).

POSITIVE MINDSET

Navigating career exploration, identifying a path, and putting your plans into action takes time, so patience and persistence are imperative. Every career journey comes with setbacks and challenges, but it is important to stay resilient and view these obstacles as opportunities for growth. Stay focused on your long-term goals while remaining adaptable to evolving circumstances. The labor market is constantly shifting, so it is crucial to stay informed on the latest trends and developments in your field and make adjustments as necessary. Flexibility and continuous learning are essential in today's rapidly changing labor market.

At times during your career journey, you may feel lost, lonely, overwhelmed, overstimulated, or exhausted. These are typical feelings! Recognize these as feelings, not as permanent states. These challenging feelings commonly arise during periods of growth, transition, or when you are pushing yourself beyond your comfort zone. These moments can be pivotal opportunities to learn, grow, and develop resilience.

Know that during your career exploration and journey you will be challenged and driven out of your comfort zone.

You will face setbacks and rejections. During discouraging moments, stay positive, reflect, regroup, and then move forward again. Below are suggestions to help you stay focused and positive during moments, days, weeks, or even years of discouragement.

Celebrate Achievements

Acknowledge and celebrate your achievements, no matter how small or big. Whether it is a small milestone or a significant accomplishment, taking time to recognize your progress can have a powerful impact on your motivation. Celebrating these wins not only boosts your confidence, but also reinforces your commitment to your long-term goals and the plan you have set in place. By recognizing your growth, you create a positive mental feedback loop that encourages continued effort and perseverance, helping you stay focused and driven as you move forward.

Work-Life Balance

As you work towards building or adjusting your career, maintain a healthy work-life balance to avoid burnout and stay motivated. While it is important to put in the effort and focus on your goals, remember that rest, self-care, and personal time are just as essential to your long-term success. Strive to find a balance that allows you to stay energized and inspired throughout your journey, without sacrificing your well-being or relationships.

Be mindful of how your career preparation fits into your life. If you are balancing multiple responsibilities—like simultaneously working, studying, while meeting personal obligations—make sure to carve out time for activities that recharge you. Overworking yourself can lead to frustration and decreased productivity. Take a break if you need to.

Seek support and advice from loved ones, mentors, or peers. Their guidance can help you stay on track and offer a sense of perspective during stressful moments. Prioritize your health and well-being while working towards your career, and you will be better equipped to handle challenges and stay motivated in the long run.

Negative Self Talk

If you experience negative self-talk or thoughts and/or imposter syndrome (the feeling that you don't deserve your success or are a "fraud," despite evidence to the contrary), it will be essential to find ways to cope with these feelings that can hinder your progress and confidence. Start by acknowledging that these are just thoughts and do not in reality define your capabilities. Challenge negative beliefs by focusing on your strengths and accomplishments, no matter how small they may seem. Reframe your mindset by viewing mistakes and setbacks as opportunities for growth rather than signs of failure. Remember that preparing for a career is a journey, and it is normal to feel uncertain at times. Be patient with yourself.

If you experience times when negative thoughts become overwhelming or persistent, affecting your mental health and progress, it may be necessary to seek professional support. While everyone can feel discouraged at times, if your feelings are hindering your ability to move forward with your career plans, causing significant stress, or leading to feelings of hopelessness, it is time to get help from a professional. A therapist or counselor can help you explore the underlying causes of these thoughts and provide strategies for managing them more effectively. Professional counseling can offer a fresh perspective, help you build resilience, and empower you to navigate your career journey with greater confidence and clarity.

Acceptance of Change

At some point on your career journey, you may realize that the path you planned no longer aligns with your goals, interests, or values, or for many other valid reasons. You might discover new passions or face unexpected challenges. These realizations may prompt a shift in your career plan. While this can be a difficult realization, it is important to accept that changing direction is a natural part of growth. Embrace the fact that as people evolve, career paths may need to change too. There is no shame in admitting that you have changed your mind. Instead of resisting the change, understand that embracing it can open doors to new opportunities that better align with you. It is okay to reassess and redirect your professional journey—it is never too late to course-correct and pursue a career that feels like a better fit for you.

Self-Awareness

Self-awareness is key to career exploration and navigating your journey. Self-awareness is not a one-time event, but rather a continuous process of checking in with yourself. It is about being honest, realistic, and intentional in evaluating your strengths, weaknesses, and circumstances.

Be honest with yourself. People frequently fall into one of two extremes when it comes to self-awareness. One group sways into the unrealistic/delusional end of the self-awareness spectrum—there is a lack of reality when it comes to their strengths, weaknesses, abilities/aptitude, and personal circumstances. The other end of the spectrum includes people who completely underestimate themself. They, too, have a false vision of reality when it comes to their strengths, weaknesses, abilities/aptitude, and personal circumstances.

Both extremes are unhelpful, as they prevent you from seeing yourself clearly. True self-awareness lies somewhere in between—acknowledging both your potential and your limitations with honesty and compassion. By staying grounded in reality, you will be better equipped to make informed decisions, set achievable goals, and navigate challenges with confidence and a clear perspective.

In Chapter 5, External Influences and Biases, you explored the various factors that may have shaped your journey so far. This involved examining your beliefs and biases which may have influenced your actions and choices up until now. Working through that chapter provides a foundation for developing honest self-awareness. The next step in this process is turning inward for a deeper self-reflection, allowing you to gain clarity and then acknowledge and understand your goals and desires, and assess how they align with your true potential.

Personal & Professional Mission

One way to start understanding your personal and professional goals is by learning to clearly express your personal and/or professional mission. Mission statements serve as a clear and concise declaration of your values, purpose, and long-term objectives. By stating what truly matters to you—whether in your career, personal life, or both—you can create a guiding framework that helps you make decisions, set priorities, and stay focused on what's most important. This statement becomes a touchstone to help you align your daily actions with your broader vision, providing both direction and motivation as you move forward.

Working in a career where your personal and professional mission are honored can significantly increase your sense of purpose at work. Having a sense of purpose is one of the largest indicators of job satisfaction and happiness. When your values align with your work, it can lead to greater fulfillment and well-being.

(For tips and suggestions on writing a personal or professional mission statement, visit msb.franklincovey.com.)

Practical v. Passion

Choosing a career requires finding a balance between pursuing your passions and considering practical factors. While it is important to follow what excites and fulfills you, it is also essential to evaluate the practical aspects of your chosen path—such as job stability, earning potential, and long-term growth opportunities. A career that aligns with your passions can provide deep satisfaction, but it is crucial to ensure that it also offers a sustainable lifestyle. Ultimately, striking this balance will help you build a career that not only inspires you, but also supports your long-term personal and financial well-being. (More on this topic in Chapter 9.)

PUTTING IN THE WORK

Mentally preparing for and navigating a career requires an unwavering commitment to hard work. Challenges and setbacks are inevitable—success rarely comes without effort or perseverance. The road ahead may be tough, but difficulty is not a reason to quit; rather, it is an opportunity to build resilience, learn, develop, and grow. Hard work is crucial to achieving lasting success and finding fulfillment in your career journey.

Continuous Learning

Continuous learning is essential throughout both your career preparation and professional journey. Embrace the opportunity to develop new skills and gain diverse experiences, as they can become invaluable assets over time. As you explore different career paths, think about the potential for both personal and professional growth. Evaluate whether the direction you're considering aligns with your long-term goals and aspirations. Additionally, in today's interconnected world, it's crucial to adopt a global perspective. Understanding international trends and cultivating a global mindset can provide a significant advantage in your chosen field.

Skill Development

To achieve professional success, it's essential to develop a balance of soft, hard, and transferable skills. Start by cultivating strong soft skills like communication, teamwork, and adaptability. These interpersonal qualities are key to thriving in any work environment, as they enable you to collaborate effectively, navigate challenges, and connect with others.

Also identify your transferable skills—those abilities that apply across multiple industries. Recognizing these skills can open up a wide range of career opportunities, giving you the flexibility to pivot and adapt to new roles with ease.

Honing your communication skills, both written and verbal, is another crucial step. Effective communication enables you to convey ideas clearly and collaborate successfully with colleagues and clients. In addition, it's important to identify the specific skills needed in your desired field and actively work on upskilling. Leverage resources like online courses, workshops, and certifications to acquire the qualifications necessary to excel.

To stay competitive in a rapidly changing labor market, adopt a mindset of continuous learning. Stay informed about industry trends, constantly update your skill set, and invest in your professional development. By blending passion with practical skills and maintaining a commitment to growth, you can build a career that is not only successful but also adaptable and resilient in the long run.

Be Teachable

Being teachable is essential throughout your career journey. Embrace, rather than resist, feedback and constructive criticism—these are both valuable tools for growth. They will help you develop and refine your skills and adapt to challenges. Being teachable will help you grow professionally and will enable you to navigate differences in the workplace more effectively, reducing the likelihood of conflict and misunderstandings.

Be teachable when it comes to staying current with technological advancements and innovations in your field. Being tech-savvy can significantly enhance your competitiveness in the labor market.

To achieve and thrive in your career, you must learn and practice appropriate workplace behaviors. Professional etiquette, such as being punctual, respectful, and mindful of workplace norms, is crucial for success. Cultivate a welcoming and inclusive mindset, embracing diversity within your team, and learn to navigate a multigenerational workforce with respect and collaboration. By staying open to learning and adapting, you position yourself for long-term success in any career.

Take Initiative

Taking initiative in your own career exploration and journey is essential—no one can, or should, do this for you. Whether in your education, training, or at work, demonstrating initiative is key to your growth and success. This means actively seeking opportunities to learn and contribute. You can show initiative by asking questions to deepen your understanding, volunteering for projects to gain experience, proposing new ideas to improve processes, and taking on additional responsibilities to demonstrate your commitment and capability.

While taking initiative can sometimes be challenging, especially when it involves stepping outside your comfort zone, it is important to push through. Putting yourself out there may not always be well-received, but don't let that stop you! Shake it off, learn from the experience, and do not let a setback deter you. Each attempt, whether successful or not, brings valuable knowledge and clarity to help you better navigate your future course.

Get to Work

Reflect on your mindset when facing challenges. What are areas that you can concentrate on when it comes to having a mindset that will contribute to your career success? How can you proactively cultivate a mindset that will contribute to your success as you navigate your career journey?

- Discuss any struggles you have with maintaining a positive mindset with someone you trust. Ask for their support in helping you regain perspective whenever you face challenges on your journey.

- Create a mission statement to help you stay aligned with what matters most to you when facing difficult decisions or challenges. What is your purpose?

- Identify areas of your life where you can take more initiative. Create a plan and take actionable steps to implement it.

Check-in

Throughout the career exploration process, mindset plays a critical role in shaping the decisions you make and how you navigate challenges. A positive mindset allows you to stay open, flexible, and adaptable, which is essential as your career path evolves. Recognize that your career may change direction over time, and that such changes are a natural part of growth. Be resilient when faced with setbacks.

Self-awareness is key to developing this mindset. By regularly checking in with yourself, you gain clarity about your strengths, weaknesses, and goals, enabling you to make informed decisions. Reflecting on both your progress and challenges also helps maintain a healthy perspective, allowing you to adjust your plans as needed without losing sight of your larger objectives.

Hard work is a fundamental part of any career journey. No path is without obstacles, and success requires perseverance, even when faced with difficulty or failure. The effort to continuously learn, adapt, and grow transforms setbacks into learning experiences and propels you toward success—helping your mindset as you navigate your career and ultimately achieve the future you desire.

Chapter Nine

Phases of Life

Depending on your phase of life and unique personal circumstances, you will need to take certain factors into account during your career decision-making process. While many common considerations apply to almost everyone, some factors may be more or less relevant to you depending on your current life stage. Although it is impossible to predict every potential variable, or define every possible "phase of life," this chapter aims to explore key considerations that may shape a career journey during different phases. Specifically, this chapter focuses on the unique challenges and opportunities that might arise depending on whether you are a high school student, a college student, someone who is underemployed or considering a career transition, or an individual reentering the workforce after taking time off.

Get Ready to Work!

This chapter covers a wide range of topics, many of which were introduced in Chapter 7, Preparation. Here, we'll dive deeper into these topics, with a focus on how they specifically relate to your current stage in life. As you read, think about your particular circumstances and phase of life, and consider how the specific advice in this chapter applies to you. Not all sections will be relevant to your situation, so focus on the ones that resonate with where you are in your life—whether you're in high school, a college student (or engaged in any variation of a degree), going through a career transition, or returning to work. Take note of the factors that apply to you. You might also find valuable insights in other sections, so feel free to browse the subsection titles to see if anything else stands out to you. (*Career Compass Workbook*, page 13.)

HIGH SCHOOL

High school students often face challenges when thinking about their future career path. By carefully considering certain factors, they can make more informed decisions, which can lead to greater personal fulfillment and long-term professional success.

Be open when it comes to considering and exploring possible career paths. You are young. You may think you know what you want to do, and you might be right. Or you may feel lost trying to navigate the possibilities that are available to you. Allow yourself time to get to know yourself, evolve, try on and try out different iterations of yourself. Do not place unnecessary pressure on yourself to know or choose your career path now. Take time to explore yourself, different ideas, possible educational opportunities, and career paths. Give yourself permission to change your mind.

One of the greatest challenges high school students face when considering their future career path is dealing with one of two situations: either there are too many options or too many obstacles. Both can make decision-making difficult, and both are valid, real challenges. However, it is possible to work through these challenges and make informed decisions that will help you reach your goals. To ensure the path you choose is the right one, it's important to understand your starting point. Gaining this clarity will provide perspective and help you anticipate obstacles that could derail your progress.

No two high school students have the same history, experiences, and personal circumstances. Therefore it can be difficult to include every possible consideration or obstacle that you may encounter at this point in your life as you consider your career choices. Thoughtfully and thoroughly consider what variables affect you. Try to understand and know how they affect you, your circumstances, thoughts, and ideas when it comes to making career choices. This should not just be a mental exercise. Talk to trusted and well informed adults in your life about your thoughts and ideas. Once you can identify your special considerations, you can problem solve or make plans to accommodate if needed.

Your age is both a gift and your greatest asset because you have time on your side—time to think, explore, plan, and take action. This gives you the freedom to shape your future without the pressure of needing immediate answers. However, with youth often comes a lack of life experience, which can make it difficult to know what factors to consider when making important career decisions. Without the real-world exposure that comes with age, it can be challenging to fully understand what all that a career path might entail. This lack of experience may leave you uncertain about how to even begin planning your career. Even though your experience may be limited, that doesn't mean you can't begin the process of discovery, growth, and informed decision-making.

Now would be a good time to refer back to Chapter 5, External Influences and Biases. Reexamine the factors that have influenced you and your life up until this point in time. Also consider any personal circumstances affecting you at the present time. Often these factors create circumstances in your life that are entirely unique to you. Identify and acknowledge anything about your personal life circumstances that should be considered as you progress through the process of exploring your possible career path.

Below are some additional areas for you to consider that will help guide you truly knowing and understand yourself before you start making important decisions that will directly impact your future.

Explore & Educate Yourself

There are several ways a high school student can explore and educate themselves to gain self-awareness from which to make informed career decisions. Start by meeting with your guidance, college, or career counselor at your school. (Another option that might be available to you through your school or school district is participation in a college and career readiness program.) Whoever you work with, ask if they have access to career assessments that you can take to help you explore your interests and what resources are available to help you learn about and explore career possibilities available to you. Make an appointment to meet one-on-one with the counselor at your school to take advantage of their expertise and knowledge and receive personal career guidance. Set up follow-up appointments as needed. (Unfortunately, many schools are understaffed or have untrained career counseling staff, which can limit the availability and/or quality of one-on-one assistance. If this is the case for you, seek other avenues for guidance.)

Another great way to explore and educate yourself while you are in high school is through work experience. Having a job provides real world experiences and valuable insights into different professions.

Additional and alternative options are participating in volunteer work, internships, job shadowing, or informational interviews. Participate in career development or career exploration days or programs available through your high school or in your community. (If you are not sure if these programs exist in your area, start by meeting with your school counselor and ask if there are any student intern partnerships or "cooperative education" opportunities that you can participate in.) Participate with curiosity and ask lots of questions. Organizers of these types of events and programs select businesses to participate that are eager to help, educate, and advise.

Often high schools host trade schools and college admission representatives. You may also have the chance to visit college campuses for tours and interviews. These can be great opportunities to explore different career and education options. Use these experiences to research the educational requirements for possible career paths.

A key part of an admission representative's job is to educate prospective students. Admission representatives should be informed about current labor market trends and predictions for the future as fields may be evolving, experiencing growth, or face challenges.

Many professions require specific degrees or certifications, and understanding these prerequisites is crucial. Whether considering attending a trade or vocational school or college/university, the representative who meets with prospective students should demonstrate a clear understanding of how their school is addressing and matching their education to the demands and changes in the current labor market.

If you know that additional schooling is not part of your future career plans, it's important to explore career options that don't require further formal education or training. However, even if high school is the end of your formal education, it's essential to understand that learning will still be a lifelong pursuit. Many careers require ongoing training, skill development, and adaptation to new tools or methods. For high school students who don't plan to continue their formal education, it's still crucial to be prepared for a future that will involve continuous learning and growth.

Many high schools offer programs aimed at making students "career ready" upon graduation. These programs can be amazing opportunities to receive formal training and earn certification and licenses in fields that will allow you to be career ready right after high school. Another possibility includes exploring the availability of dual degree programs, in which you are concurrently enrolled in high school and community college. These programs allow students to graduate from high school with a high school diploma and an associate degree at the same time. Typically, these programs are offered at little or no cost to the students.

Passions & Practicality

When exploring career options, it's important to find a balance between following your passions and being practical. While your interests are a key factor in choosing a career, they are not always the same as your passions, and those passions might change over time. Be aware that compromise may be necessary as you navigate this process.

As you explore different options, it's crucial to weigh personal fulfillment against practical considerations. Strive to balance pursuing what you love with making practical choices, and thoroughly research both aspects during your decision-making process. It's also important to recognize that passions evolve over time. Some passions may fade, while new ones may emerge as you grow. Basing your career choice solely on passion can sometimes create blind spots. For example, what if there's little demand for your passion in the labor market? Additionally, many people find that when a passion becomes a job, their feeling for it changes. This shift can happen due to the increased frequency of exposure to the passion, or because working for money can alter the relationship you have with the thing you once loved.

Conversely, choosing a career based purely on practicality can also lead to difficulties. Just because a career looks good on paper—seemingly the best option, the easiest choice, or the most logical—doesn't mean it will meet all the personal and professional needs you might have. When evaluating practical options, be sure to thoughtfully weigh them against other factors that matter to you, and consider whether they will ultimately lead to both professional success and personal fulfillment.

Lifestyle

High school is a good time to begin considering the work-life balance associated with different career options. Some professions may demand long hours, irregular schedules, or travel. It is essential to align career choices with your personal preferences. Determining how you feel about these factors may be difficult unless you have actually experienced them to some degree. Often we can romanticize the idea of travel or not consider the toll of working long or irregular hours. Or, you may assume you have a strong aversion to something when in fact you don't know because you have never tried it. When researching career options, seriously consider the lifestyle implications of each career choice. Once again, work, internships, informational interviews, and job shadowing each provide opportunities to see and experience what the demands are of different careers.

Lifestyle and career choices may also require factoring in geography. Certain jobs or industries may require living in a particular location. Consider if you are willing to relocate, and the various ways that may impact you. If you know that relocation will be required based on certain career choices, include in your research the areas where you may end up living to ensure you will be happy living wherever those options may take you.

Often lifestyle is an area where there can be adjustments, changes, or flexibility once you have established yourself in your career. It is important to be fully informed of all of the lifestyle ramifications your career choices will have on your future as you are exploring your career choices.

Family

Your family circumstances are completely unique to you. You know what they are since you've been living with and through them. Thoughtfully consider how your family circumstances are going to change once you are no longer in high school. Understand what your financial and housing situation will be after you graduate. This may require having some hard and candid conversations about expectations and reality; what can you reasonably expect and what is the reality of your situation as it relates to your family as you move forward. What you learn could affect your career choices.

Preferences & Aversions

It is normal to have preferences and aversions when it comes to careers. Do not judge yourself based on their "validity," or let other people's opinions sway you.

However, please try to understand that at this time in your life you may not be aware of all of your preferences or aversions, and it is also possible that they may change with time, exposure, and experience.

Take the time to understand and know your preferences and aversions when exploring career options. You may find that knowing your aversions will be an easy way to eliminate possibilities. When individuals are struggling to identify what possible careers they might want to pursue, it is sometimes helpful to list out what they don't want to do to gain perspective on what areas are left remaining.

Fear & Self Doubt

As you navigate new and unexpected experiences, you'll encounter many unknowns. It's natural for these challenges to bring up feelings of fear and self-doubt. Feeling this way during the transition to life after high school is completely normal. Preparation can help ease your fears and self-doubt, but the main thing to remember is that it's okay to feel uncomfortable. (Please take a moment to really absorb this: It is okay to feel uncomfortable!)

What is a total distraction and can delay your quest is letting discomfort, fear, or self-doubt paralyze you, control you, or throw you off track. Make plans, push forward, and know that you will survive. The sense of accomplishment and pride you'll feel from confronting your fears and facing the unknown will build your confidence and strengthen your resolve as you work toward the life you want to create.

Also, give yourself permission to start a career and change your mind later. Give yourself a break with self permission to learn, grow, and make adjustments as needed. Do not be afraid to try again!

Outside Influences

You may encounter a lot of well-meaning people at this stage in your life that want to give you advice. The reality is that some of their advice is good, maybe even great. But some of it could also be not-so-great, or even bad advice.

Keep in mind this perspective as you hear their advice and decide what weight you should give it. Is the person offering their advice telling you what they wish they had known when they were in your position? Is their advice based on their life experiences and their own personal circumstances? In these circumstances, the advice may or may not translate perfectly to you, because your experiences and circumstances are different from theirs.

My recommendation is to hear them out, offer your gratitude for their thoughtfulness and caring enough about you to share their ideas. Then think about and decide if, what, and how you will apply the advice they offered you.

Pressure

Do not put unnecessary pressure on yourself to decide your future when you are in high school. Not knowing, being undecided, having too many ideas, not having any clue, are all perfectly normal feelings, especially at this phase in your life. The truth is, even the most educated people and seasoned professionals still experience many of these same feelings with regards to their career. Take the pressure off yourself to make a decision, and replace it with a commitment to intentionally and thoroughly explore your options.

You will be asked countless times as you approach the end of high school, "What do you want to be?" It is absolutely okay to not know, and to respond accordingly. Do not let the frequency of this question pressure you to make a decision so that you have a response in order to avoid feeling awkward. Uncertainty about what path you should choose for your future is normal. Construct a response that you are comfortable with explaining what you are doing to explore and learn about your options.

Choosing a Post-Secondary Option

"Post-secondary" refers to any education that takes place after high school. This includes a variety of institutions and programs, such as colleges and universities (both in-person and online), community or junior college, trade and vocational schools, apprenticeship programs, continuing education programs, art and design schools, language schools, military academies, and employer-sponsored specialized training or certification programs.

The college you choose can either expand or limit your career opportunities, depending on the academic programs and experiences it offers. While factors such as size, prestige, location, athletics, Greek life, and financial considerations can certainly influence your decision, it is crucial to be honest with yourself about what's truly guiding your choice. These aspects may enhance your overall college experience, but they shouldn't overshadow the importance of selecting a school that provides the academic tracks and resources that align with your career goals. Focusing too heavily on non-academic factors can lead to frustration if, after enrolling, you discover the school doesn't offer the degree or program you need to pursue your chosen path, forcing you to either compromise when selecting a school or scramble for alternative majors. Ultimately, the academic opportunities should be the top priority, as they directly shape your future career prospects.

I want to reassure you that it is perfectly okay to start college, even if you are not exactly sure what career you want to pursue yet. Many students begin college with a few ideas or possibilities, and that is completely normal. Make sure that the college you choose offers resources like career counseling, internships, and mentorship programs to help you explore different career paths within majors and beyond graduation.

College is a time for personal growth and discovery, and there are plenty of opportunities to discover and learn things as you go that will refine your career exploration. There are often hundreds, if not more, possible career paths for each major, so even if you don't have a specific career in mind right now, your college experience can still be incredibly valuable. Exploring different options, gaining new skills, and discovering your interests along the way will help you shape your future, even if the exact path isn't clear at the start. College is not just about landing a job; it is about preparing yourself for the countless opportunities that will unfold as you grow and learn. (Read the COLLEGE STUDENTS section below for additional advice.)

Gap Year

Many high school students consider taking a gap year after graduation and before starting college. While a gap year can offer numerous benefits, it also presents certain challenges that should be carefully weighed.

A gap year can be a valuable opportunity if used intentionally. For instance, it can help you explore your interests, allowing you to discover what subjects you might want to study or what type of work you might enjoy. It can also provide a chance to earn money, which could help reduce the financial burden of college by allowing you to pay for tuition and other expenses in cash, rather than relying on student loans. Additionally, a gap year gives you time to reflect and gain clarity about your future, including decisions about education and career. However, it is important to acknowledge that even after taking this time you may still face uncertainty about your next steps.

One of the main dangers and major concerns when it comes to taking a gap year, is that it can turn into a prolonged break without producing any meaningful direction. This can cause you to lose momentum and struggle to reintegrate into an academic setting later on. Without a clear purpose during a gap year, it can easily slip into a year of inactivity, poor decision-making, or lack of structure, which can delay your educational and career goals.

A gap year should not be seen as simply a "break" or an excuse to avoid the responsibilities of school or work. It is not a time for endless relaxation or aimless travel without a sense of purpose. If you choose to take a gap year, it should be a deliberate and productive period.

If you choose to take a gap year, it is crucial to have a well-structured plan in place. Set specific goals and objectives to ensure that you make the most of your time. While taking time to "find yourself" can be an enriching experience, it is important to approach it with purpose. Work intentionally toward personal growth by creating a clear roadmap for your gap year that aligns with your long-term goals. This might include internships, volunteering, informational interviews, job shadowing, or part- and full-time work.

You might also want to consider taking a couple of classes at a community college during your gap year. This can be a good way to get some of your non-major/prerequisite classes completed. Also consider enrolling in a career exploration class.

However you choose to spend your gap year, having a clear objectives and direction is essential. Thoughtfully consider your options. Discuss your ideas and plans with someone who you can hold you accountable to ensure your objectives are met.

COLLEGE STUDENTS

This section may require some flexibility in understanding and applying the categories that relate to your specific situation. One of the challenges in writing this for college students is addressing the wide range of needs across different types of students, from the "traditional college student" (someone who enrolls full-time immediately after high school) to the many variations of the "non-traditional college student." Regardless of your age, whether you're a full-time or part-time student, or the type of college you're enrolled in, your school should offer a variety of resources to support your career exploration and planning. Make sure to seek out and take full advantage of these resources.

Often, your academic path is set when you apply to college, and you arrive with a decision already made. If you're comfortable with that decision, feel free to stick with it. However, if you arrive undecided or find yourself second-guessing your choice along the way, make use of the resources your school offers to help guide you.

Many people attend college before knowing what career they want to pursue. Selecting a college major is incredibly important and can be an extremely difficult decision for any person to make. In a traditional college setting, the first two years of college often involve completing core classes or prerequisites, leaving little time to explore all available fields. Ultimately, every college major can lead to hundreds of different career paths, so there's no need to rush into a decision. Take time to explore, as many people attend college without knowing exactly what career they want to pursue.

Similar to the discussion earlier in the HIGH SCHOOL section of this chapter, taking a gap year in college can be a valuable option if you're still struggling to decide on your academic or career path. It provides time to step back, gain real-world experience, and explore different interests without the pressure of school. Whether through internships, work opportunities, or volunteer experiences, a gap year can offer new perspectives and help you clarify your goals. By immersing yourself in different environments, you may gain a clearer sense of direction, allowing you to make more informed decisions when you return to your studies.

Use the additional resources at your college or university to explore as many majors as you can. Take advantage of all the opportunities your school provides to explore different majors. Many school websites offer information on career prospects for each major. If not, or in addition to this, meet with faculty members and have thorough, in-depth conversations about career options available to you after graduation, based on your education and qualifications. Meet with professors during office hours and seek their advice and expertise. Your school should also have academic advisors and a career development center where you can receive advice and guidance. Attend career and networking events hosted on campus. Come prepared to these events to ask plenty of questions. Listen and learn.

Career Office

Every college should have a "career office" that provides free (or low cost) resources to their enrolled student body. The name of the office will be different at each school. Some possibilities are: Career Development, Career Services, Career Center, Career Advising, Career Placement, Professional Development, Career Education, Success and Achievement Services, Internship and Career Planning Office, or Center for Career Readiness. (For simplicity, it will subsequently be referred to as a career office.) Locate the career office at your college and identify what services they provide. This can be done from reviewing their webpage on the college's website, or stopping by their office and asking them in person about their services. Below are a list of services that can be extremely beneficial to you in your career exploration while in college. Some of the ways that your career office should be of assistance are:

- Career Assessments. Your school's career office likely offers free access to various career assessment tools (many of which were outlined in Chapter 6, Assessment Tools). Please do not base your career choice solely on the results of one career assessment. Instead, consider these tools as just one piece of your overall career planning.

- Job Shadowing & Internships. Gain practical experience through job shadowing, internships, or even part-time work. Real-world exposure helps students understand the industry, make informed decisions, and—as a bonus—enhance their resumes. Many schools have internship coordinators who can help facilitate these experiences and opportunities.

- Career Exploration Events. Take the time to explore and research various careers. Understanding the day-to-day responsibilities, job outlook, and growth potential in different fields is essential for making informed decisions. Attend career fairs, participate in department events, and engage in career education seminars to gain valuable insights and connect with professors/instructors in your areas of interest.

- Career Tools. Part of the services provided by the career office should also include assistance with job searching, writing resumes and cover letters, job interviewing preparation, creating your professional branding including your online professional social networking presence on LinkedIn or your own website/portfolio. Do some research to find out how long you have access to these services provided at the career office at your school. (Some schools continue to provide these services indefinitely to their alumni.)

- Career Planning Workshop/Class. Consider enrolling in a career planning workshop or class if your school offers one.

Author's Note

If your college's career office is lacking in resources or does a poor job of providing support, you have a legitimate reason to be concerned. The services and support from the career office are part of what you are counting on when you choose a school. Career services are a crucial resource for successfully gaining employment, and if the school's offerings don't meet your needs or expectations, you may not be getting the full value of your education. Be sure to research the quality of your college's career services before committing and financially investing your time and energy into a program that may not help you achieve your career goals.

Academic Planning

Depending on your school, the academic planning/advising department may or may not be part of the career office. If they aren't partnered together (and many are not), they should still collaborate closely to help students align their academic goals with their career aspirations. Upon enrollment, you should be assigned, or allowed to choose, an academic advisor. The role of an academic advisor is to help you create a course schedule that ensures you stay on track for graduation. Additionally, academic advisors should be familiar with the majors, programs, and career paths available at your school and guide you in navigating your course load to achieve both your academic and professional goals.

If you haven't already chosen a major, your academic advisor can assist with that as well. As mentioned in the previous HIGH SCHOOL section, under Selecting a College/University, there are often hundreds, if not more, potential career paths for each major. Make sure to utilize the resources available through both the academic advising and/or the career office to explore all the opportunities open to you through your school.

While every school is different, most academic advisors will not provide advice beyond your specific academic needs. They will help you navigate your academic progress at the college based on your academic and career goals. But they will not help you decide on what those goals are, or should be. Much of this type of advising is outside the scope of an academic advisor's job responsibilities (and professional training). Assistance in reaching your career goals should come from qualified staff in the career office or through the exploratory services and events offered by your college.

Networking

Take advantage of the different networking opportunities offered at your college. Thoughtfully explore and consider what opportunities you will want to invest your time and attention to. Many lifelong personal connections are formed and built during and through your college. Some of the sources for networking at a college and university are your classmates, professors/instructors, alumni networks, studying abroad, clubs, activities, and Greek life. Seek out and participate in opportunities at your school that will allow you to build a personal network and seek mentorship. Connect with individuals in your desired field as it can provide insights, advice, and potential opportunities. School alumni associations and many Greek life organizations often continue to provide valuable networking support and opportunities even after graduation.

On-Campus Work Opportunities

Real-world work experience is a great way to help college students understand career industries, make informed decisions, and enhance their resumes. Therefore it can be extremely beneficial to gain and participate in on-campus employment opportunities. Any and all hands-on work experience, whether paid or unpaid, allows students to apply what they've learned in class in a real-world context. These experiences can provide them with a clearer sense of what career paths they might want to pursue. Some various ways to "work" on campus include:

- Often professors hire research students to work for them on research, which can involve assisting on academic research projects. While the job roles can vary depending on the discipline, and type of research, students may have the opportunity to participate in tasks like data collection, literature reviews, laboratory work, conducting experiments, analyzing results, or even assisting with writing research papers. This can result in academic and professional growth opportunities, skill development, mentorship, the possibility of academic publications, and/or attending academic conferences.

- On-campus jobs can be an effective way to gain work experience that can help students discern the type of work or work environment they enjoy (or want to avoid in the future).

- Many unpaid work experiences offer valuable work experience. Seek out leadership roles in student-led activities and organizations.

CAREER TRANSITION

Making a career transition can be both challenging and rewarding. While most career changes involve uncertainty and difficulty, they also offer opportunities for growth and reinvention. As you consider shifting careers, it's important to stay open to learning, recognize that adapting to new environments may take time, and remain resilient in the face of setbacks. Transitioning careers may require not only acquiring new skills but also adjusting to a different workplace culture, which can bring both exciting opportunities and challenges. Therefore, it's essential to carefully consider how this change might impact all areas of your life—personal, financial, and professional.

Reasons for considering a career transition include underemployment, economic shifts, personal or family changes, or simply a desire for greater career satisfaction. As you research potential new careers, it is crucial to evaluate how they fit with your work-life balance. Ask yourself whether the new roles you are considering align with your personal values, long-term goals, and lifestyle preferences. When contemplating a career change, you will need to spend time researching different possible fields. It is just as important to research yourself. Reflect on your skills, interests, and non-negotiables, and consider how these factors will influence your decision.

Be sure to consider all the various financial factors that may affect your decisions. A career transition can impact your income, savings, and overall financial security. Assess how the change might affect your earnings in both the short and long term. This may involve budgeting for a potential pay cut or considering whether you need to invest in additional training or education. Understanding the financial implications of a career transition will help you make informed decisions and create a strategy that can minimize unnecessary stress.

Identify Motivation

Identify your motivation for a career change. This is important to ensure that the outcome aligns with your true goals and desires. If you switch careers without fully understanding the reasons behind your need for change, you risk making a move that could ultimately leave you feeling even more dissatisfied or stuck. It is crucial to clearly identify what is driving your decision—whether it is a lack of fulfillment, a desire for new challenges, a shift in personal values, or something else entirely. Understanding your underlying motivations will give you clarity and purpose, helping to guide your decision-making process.

To gain clarity on your motivation for a career change, have open conversations with people you trust and respect. You could talk to your parents or loved ones, as they often have a deep understanding of your personality, strengths, and goals, and can offer valuable perspectives. A mentor, whether from your current field or an entirely different industry, can provide insight into how your skills might transfer and help you explore new career possibilities.

Sometimes, speaking with a therapist can be incredibly helpful, especially if your desire for a career change stems from personal or emotional challenges. A therapist can guide you through self-reflection and help you understand any deeper motivations or fears. Additionally, consider talking to peers or colleagues who have gone through similar transitions—they can offer practical advice and share their own experiences. By gathering feedback from a range of sources, you can better understand your own desires and make a more informed, thoughtful decision about your career path.

When you have a clear understanding about why you want to make a change, it not only provides you with the necessary motivation to take the leap, but it also strengthens your resolve to follow through with the career transition, when challenges arise. Being able to articulate your reasons for the career change will serve as a powerful reminder of your goals, helping you stay focused and navigate potential setbacks. Ultimately, knowing why you are making the change will empower you to make more informed decisions, setting you up for a more successful and fulfilling career path in the long run.

Self Assessment

A thorough self-assessment can help you understand the reasons behind your desire for a career change, as well as guide you in making informed and intentional decisions. Several key areas are necessary to consider during this process, along with a variety of tools to assist you:

- Reflecting on your values, interests, and long-term goals. This will provide clarity and confidence as you navigate your transition.

- Assess your current skills, strengths, and personal interests.

- Identifying your transferable skills—those that can be applied across different industries or roles—will open up a wider range of career options. Recognizing these skills will help you see how your experience can be valuable in new contexts, making the transition smoother.

- Identify any skill gaps—areas where further development is needed to pivot successfully into a new field. Understanding these gaps will allow you to prioritize the skills you need to acquire, whether through additional training, education, or hands-on experience.

Career assessments can also be useful for those considering a career change. If you're uncertain about which direction to take, these tools can provide insights by suggesting paths that align with your strengths and interests. They can also help confirm whether your chosen direction is a good fit for your interests, skills, and values. In this way, assessments act as a guide, ensuring that the changes you are planning will lead to a fulfilling and sustainable career. Whether you're exploring new options or validating your chosen path, career assessments can provide the clarity you need to make confident decisions (Chapter 6, Assessment Tools).

Career Tools

When considering a career change, it is essential to plan to develop your career tools across all key areas, including the online application process, resumes, cover letters, and networking. Tailor your resume and online profiles, such as LinkedIn, to highlight your relevant skills, experiences, and accomplishments that align with your new target industry. It is also important to develop a compelling narrative that explains your career transition in a positive and relatable way, demonstrating how your past experiences make you a strong candidate for your new role.

Networking plays a critical role in a successful career transition. It is important to inform your colleagues, friends, family, and mentors about your plans and aspirations, but be strategic about when and with whom you share your intentions. Use discretion, as timing and context can influence the response you receive. Leverage both your personal and professional networks before and during the transition to seek advice, gain insights, and uncover potential job opportunities. Don't underestimate the power of word-of-mouth. Sometimes, the right connection can lead to unexpected opportunities. Continue to network even after the transition, as building and maintaining strong relationships is essential for long-term career success. Remember, networking is not just about finding a job; it is about cultivating meaningful relationships that provide guidance, collaboration, and ongoing support throughout your career.

Research

Researching the labor market is an essential step in preparing for a successful career transition. Start by identifying industries and roles with strong demand and growth potential, considering factors such as salary, job satisfaction, and work-life balance. Stay informed about industry trends and developments. This will help you align your skills with current industry needs and better understand what employers are looking for in job candidates. Additionally, consider whether a mentor in your desired field could offer valuable guidance.

In some cases, consulting a career counselor can also be beneficial. Career counselors, while often available to high school and college students, can also be hired by professionals making a career shift. They can assist you in administering assessments (such as personality or interest tests), identifying transferable skills, and exploring potential career paths. Some career counselors can also help you develop a job search strategy, provide emotional support through any anxieties you may experience during the transition, and assist with career tools like resumes and cover letters. By combining your own research with expert advice, you'll be better equipped to make informed decisions and successfully navigate your career transition.

Professional Development

Invest in yourself and seek out and engage in professional development opportunities. This is one of the most valuable steps you can take during a career transition. If available, take full advantage of professional development resources within your current organization or employer. Many companies offer perks such as tuition reimbursement, paid training, and internal development programs. These opportunities are designed as an incentive for employees and helps their workforce acquire new skills, improve job performance, and advance within the organization. By taking advantage of these offerings, you can sharpen your skills and demonstrate your commitment to continuous growth.

Outside of your current employer, it is important to proactively seek additional opportunities to expand your knowledge and expertise. Attend workshops, enroll in online courses, participate in training programs, and attend industry conferences to stay ahead of the curve. Gain new certifications or specialized skills relevant to your desired career path. This will build your confidence and reinforce your decision to pursue this new trajectory. Engaging in these development activities can deepen your understanding of your chosen field and solidify your commitment to the career change.

Hands-on experience is crucial for testing the waters and ensuring that your chosen field aligns with your long-term goals. Look for opportunities such as internships, freelance work, volunteering, or part-time positions in your desired field. These experiences will provide valuable insights into day-to-day responsibilities, help you build a professional network, and enhance your marketability when you eventually transition into your new career. Other ways to explore the field include informational interviews and job shadowing, which can give you an inside look at what working in a particular role or industry truly entails. Every opportunity to gain real-world exposure will help you make a more informed decision. (It can also strengthen your resume!)

In addition to in-person opportunities, consider exploring online learning platforms like Coursera, Udemy, and edX, which offer a wide range of courses and certifications across various industries. These platforms provide flexible learning schedules, allowing you to gain knowledge at your own pace while balancing your other responsibilities. MasterClass also offers courses taught by experts in fields ranging from business to creative arts, providing an opportunity to learn directly from top industry leaders. By combining formal and informal learning experiences, you can build a broad skill set that will support your career transition.

Transition Plan

Transition Plan is synonymous with Career Plan, a topic covered in more detail in Chapter 14. (In the *Career Compass Workbook*, the Career Plan template on pages 23–24 can also be used to create a Transition Plan.) Having a transition plan is essential to develop a detailed guide through the process of shifting careers. A transition plan serves as a strategic roadmap, helping you navigate the complexities of moving from one career path to another. Just like any Career Plan, a transition plan should be broken down into short-term, mid-term, and long-term goals, with clear action steps outlined for each stage.

Your transition plan should be flexible enough to adapt to unexpected challenges or new opportunities. It is important to regularly reassess your progress and make adjustments as needed. By having a clear, structured plan, you can approach your career transition with confidence, staying focused and motivated as you move toward your new professional goals.

RETURN TO WORK

Regardless of the reasons for your time away from the workforce or the duration of your absence, returning to meaningful and gainful employment is always possible. However, it is important to recognize that re-entering the workforce may present unique challenges. With thoughtful research and careful planning, you can make this transition smoother and more successful, ultimately achieving your employment and career goals.

You may find it helpful to review the CAREER TRANSITION section above to identify any relevant information that could assist you in your journey. Additionally, consider the following key factors as you plan for a successful return to work.

Research

Researching the current labor market is essential to understand how trends, job requirements, and industry expectations may have evolved during your time away from work. Industries can change rapidly, and it is important to identify how advancements or shifts in technology, regulations, or practices could affect your field. Be mindful of emerging roles, new skills in demand, and any evolving standards that may impact your career prospects.

When considering your return to work, it's important to evaluate your career ideas against what is realistically available in the labor market. Think about what you want to do, but also take the time to assess what opportunities currently exist within your areas of interest. By understanding the current demands and available roles, you can better align your skills with what employers are looking for and tailor your job search to increase your chances of success. This approach will help you make more informed decisions, setting you up for a smoother and more effective transition back to work.

Self Assessment

Identify your unique circumstances to gain clarity on how your return to work may be influenced by personal factors. Your employment gap could be linked to various aspects of your life, such as physical health, family responsibilities, or financial considerations. Each person's situation is entirely unique, and understanding the factors that have shaped your career break is crucial for planning a successful return to work. Take time to evaluate where you are now, what challenges or resources may be at play, and how these will need to be addressed as you prepare to re-enter the workforce. For instance, if family commitments or health concerns have been central to your time away, think about how you can integrate these needs into your work-life balance moving forward.

Assess your current marketable skills. Reflect on the abilities you have developed through various experiences, such as previous education or training, work experience, or even unpaid or volunteer work. Consider how these skills are transferable to the labor market and which ones align with the demands of your desired career field. Transferable skills, like communication, problem-solving, project management, or technical proficiencies, are valuable assets that can help you bridge the gap between your past roles and your new career direction. By evaluating your skill set and identifying areas that may need further development, you can take targeted steps to ensure your skills are aligned with current industry needs.

Update Skills & Training

After evaluating your current marketable skills, consider which ones may need updating or additional training to align with current industry demands. Depending on your specific circumstances, it may be necessary to start small. Explore part-time roles, internships, or volunteer opportunities to gain hands-on experience. Volunteering or taking on part-time work related to your field of interest can provide valuable exposure and help you build recent work experience that will strengthen your resume. If formal education is required to upgrade your skills, consider enrolling in classes through an adult education center, community college, or online platforms.

Career Tools

Much of the guidance around career tools has already been covered in the CAREER TRANSITION section under Career Tools, but a few unique aspects need special attention to effectively utilize your tools, particularly when addressing employment gaps. For example, when updating your resume, cover letter, and preparing for job interviews, it is essential to clearly address any gaps in your employment history.

Tailor your resume to highlight the relevant skills and experiences that align with your new target industry. Focus on your transferable skills and how they can be applied to the roles you are pursuing. Craft a compelling cover letter that not only addresses your employment gap but also emphasizes how your experiences during the gap have helped develop valuable skills. Ensure your cover letter can be easily adapted to various job applications, clearly linking your background to the employer's needs. Additionally, develop a narrative to explain your return to work in the best possible light. Update your LinkedIn profile and other professional online platforms. Showcase your skills, experiences, and any relevant achievements. While preparing for interviews, practice responding to questions concerning your gap. Be ready to articulate how your time away from the workforce has equipped you with new skills or perspectives that are valuable to the employer.

Networking plays a crucial role in facilitating your return to work. Reconnect with former colleagues, mentors, and industry contacts. Networking can provide valuable insights, job leads, and recommendations. Reach out and let prior contacts know about your intention to return to work. Ask for their advice on navigating a return, especially if you are re-entering an industry they're still active in. Attend networking events and industry-related gatherings to expand your professional network. Build confidence in asking questions and making meaningful connections. Cultivating strong relationships can open doors to job opportunities and provide valuable guidance during your transition.

Build a personal support system by surrounding yourself with a network of people who can offer encouragement and practical support. Share your thoughts and plans with family and friends, as their emotional support can help you stay motivated. Mentorship is also invaluable; seek out professionals in your field of interest who can offer advice, share their own experiences, and guide you through industry-specific challenges.

Mindset

Returning to the workforce can be tricky mentally. Understanding this will help you maintain a positive mindset throughout the process. Your job search might not be quick, and it is important to stay patient, persistent, and focused on your long-term goals. Set realistic expectations for the application and hiring process. You may encounter setbacks that lead you to question your abilities or your chances of success. During these times, it is essential to stay flexible and open to various opportunities. Consider roles that can serve as stepping stones back into your desired field, even if they aren't the exact position you initially envisioned.

Understand that adjusting to a new career or re-entering the workforce may take time. Be patient with yourself and the process. Focus your mindset on the skills and experiences that make you a valuable asset to employers, rather than fixating on what you might feel is lacking.

You have a unique set of skills and experiences that make you a valuable employee. Keep that in mind, and carry that confidence with you as you navigate your career return.

Get to Work

Think about what are your particular circumstances and motivations for exploring your career options? What are areas where you can prepare yourself that will contribute to your career success? (*Career Compass Workbook*, page 13.)

- What are your unique circumstances based on your phase of life?

- How do you plan to accommodate your circumstances during your career exploration?

- What research do you need to do to be prepared to make educated and informed career decisions? (Start doing that research now!)

Check-in

Thoughtfully consider your unique circumstances and phase of life in shaping your career decisions. Whether you are in high school, college, contemplating a career transition, or reentering the workforce, understanding factors that impact you will help you make informed, realistic choices.

Part 2: Recap
Additional Considerations

When exploring career options, it is essential to consider the unique personal circumstances that apply specifically to you at the present time. Your life situation—whether it involves health, family, financial concerns, or other factors—can significantly influence your career decisions. These nuances are often not fully understood or accounted for by external advisers or career assessments. By taking the time to reflect on and evaluate these additional considerations, you will be better equipped to make informed, thoughtful decisions about your career path.

This section of the book led you through three key areas for consideration during your career exploration— preparation, mindset, and stages of life—that can help you identify and understand the factors that should shape your decision-making process.

In order to create that plan, you will need to focus on research, networking, career tools, and understand your financial circumstances to ensure you are fully prepared. Your mindset plays a pivotal role in this process, so staying open, flexible, and adaptable will serve you well as you encounter challenges and opportunities along the way. Remember, your career path is not set in stone; it is natural for plans to evolve.

Part 3 - Explore Options

Chapter Ten

Finances

Consider your financial goals and the lifestyle you desire. Be honest with yourself about the expectations and desires you have for your future life. It is important to understand and acknowledge that your income will determine nearly every aspect of your life, such as housing, transportation, savings, travel, overall lifestyle, and retirement. Understanding what it costs to live is essential for making educated and well-informed decisions regarding which career choices will enable you to meet your financial goals and lifestyle. Carefully consider how you want to balance career satisfaction with financial considerations. While income is important, it is equally crucial to find a career that aligns with your strengths, interests, values, and goals.

There are many useful online resources available to research salaries for different careers and industries. While researching income, be aware that salaries can vary depending upon work experience, education, and geographic location. It is also important to understand how entry-level salaries will increase with potential advancement opportunities. Knowledge of entry-level salaries can be just as important as understanding long-term earning potential.

Author's Note

Your focus on finances may vary depending on where you are in life. For example, what a high school student considers adequate may be quite different from a working professional contemplating a career change. Additionally, a high school student's knowledge and awareness of the cost of living will differ from that of an experienced professional. Consider how to adapt this research to your financial situation.

Get Ready to Work!

Assess different financial implications of potential career choices—cost of living, income, and return on investment. The research suggestions and tools outlined in this chapter are intended to help you make informed financial decisions as you evaluate career options. Before you begin your research, decide which areas and factors are most relevant to you. Use the *Career Compass Workbook* to record your thoughts, ideas, and research (pages 15–17.)

COST OF LIVING

It is important to compare the potential salary of a career to cost of living. This comparison will help you determine the financial viability of your career options. With this knowledge, you can make a well-informed decision about whether a career is likely to provide you with the future you desire. Evaluating the financial implications of a career in relation to where you might live is crucial when deciding which career path is right for you.

Two helpful websites for researching the cost of living are the U.S. Census Bureau (census.gov) and the MIT Living Wage Calculator (livingwage.mit.edu). These sites provide valuable information on what constitutes a livable wage and the median household income in different geographic areas. Be aware of geographic variations in salaries, as they can fluctuate based on the cost of living in different regions. It may also be important to consider whether you are open to relocation and where you would be willing to live, as these factors can impact your earning potential.

The MIT Living Wage Calculator provides information that "families and individuals working in low-wage jobs make too little income to meet minimum standards of living in their community. We developed the Living Wage Calculator to help individuals, communities, employers, and others estimate the local wage rate that a full-time worker requires to cover the costs of their family's basic needs where they live. Explore the living wage in your county, metro area, or state for 12 different family types." The website offers easy-to-navigate data by state and county.

The U.S. Census Bureau provides information on livable wages associated with different career options in various forms. It offers data on income levels, cost of living, occupational trends, demographic factors, geographic variations, and trends over time. With this information, you can effectively assess the financial viability of various career choices and make strategic decisions to support your goals and lifestyle desires.

Below is a list of specific pages to help narrow down search criteria for areas of interest related to income, household, and employment data:

- Income Data: census.gov/topics/income-poverty /income/news-updates/updates.html

- Median Household Income Data:
  census.gov/quickfacts/fact/map/
  atlantacitygeorgiaUS/INC110221

- Employment Data:
  census.gov/topics/employment.html

You may want to evaluate factors such as housing, transportation, healthcare, food, and taxes. Keep in mind that the cost of living can vary significantly between geographic areas. Websites like Numbeo (numbeo.com), Expatistan (expatistan.com), and BestPlaces (bestplaces.net) offer tools to compare the costs between cities and regions, providing valuable insight into how the cost of living differs from place to place.

Understanding the cost of living in your chosen location will also allow you to assess whether a particular career path can support your personal and professional aspirations in the long term. For more detailed comparisons, you can also use tools from the Economic Policy Institute (epi.org) to evaluate cost differences in the U.S., taking into account factors like family income and overall expenses.

Use these resources to determine what you can reasonably expect the cost of living to be in the area where you plan to live and work. Pay attention to how different cities and states may affect your financial situation. Knowing your cost of living will give you a clearer picture of how your potential salary might align with your lifestyle and financial goals.

Income

For most people, their primary reason to work is to generate an income. Your income will determine whether you can meet your short- and long-term financial goals.

Whether it is saving for a home, starting a family, or retiring comfortably, ensure that your career path supports these objectives.

O*Net is an excellent tool to quickly research salary information for specific careers. Each career listed on O*Net provides salary data for the US, as well as for state and local areas. When you are on the page for the career you are researching, scroll down (or use the Contents button) to the Workforce Characteristics section. Listed under Wage & Employment Trends are the national median wages for the career, both hourly and annually. In this section, income can also be searched by state and local wages.

Workforce Characteristics

Wages & Employment Trends

Median wages (2023)	$29.61 hourly, $61,590 annual
State wages	Alabama ∨ Go
Local wages	ZIP Code Go
Employment (2023)	779,800 employees
Projected growth (2023-2033)	■■■■ Much faster than average (9% or higher)
Projected job openings (2023-2033)	80,200
State trends	Alabama ∨ Go
Top industries (2023)	Construction

You can use several other online resources to conduct salary research. Simply type into Google: "What is the average income for a _____ in _____?"

The website Glassdoor (glassdoor.com) can also be useful for researching salaries within specific companies. Reviewing current job postings can give you a good idea of the expected salary range that employers are offering.

Whatever method you use, it is important to research job postings in different geographical areas. Understanding salary ranges and being informed can help you make a well-considered decision about your career choice. It will also benefit you in the future as a job seeker by giving you previous knowledge to make informed decisions about where you want to work, live, and what is reasonable to expect for compensation.

Some additional variables to consider when accurately learning about the potential income of a career include irregular earnings, overtime, and commission or performance-based-pay. Careers that fall into freelance or entrepreneurial fields can be difficult to assess and predict for earning potential. While these career paths can offer great financial rewards, know that these rewards need to be balanced with potential financial risks. Some careers offer a typical work schedule and pay, but also provide the potential for overtime, resulting in even greater earnings.

Consider your work-life balance for careers with long additional hours in exchange for extra income. Often, the overtime hours and pay will require working nights, weekends, and/or holidays. Commission based careers may result in a variable income based on your performance and goal achievement. Commission earnings are meant to motivate employees by increasing income with performance, but they can lead to an income that is difficult to predict and may be affected by factors outside your control.

Financial Planning

Consider creating a financial plan that includes a budget and your savings goals. This can be a valuable tool for gaining perspective on your short- and long-term financial priorities. Be mindful of your specific financial goals.

Financial stability provides greater flexibility in career choices and may offer opportunities to adjust or redirect your career path in the future, if desired. You may want to plan to save a certain amount of money based on the total cost of a potential degree. Use this research to create a realistic budget that factors in all anticipated expenses. Be sure to include one-time costs or recurring expenses throughout the duration of your training or education, such as additional courses, tests, certifications, or licensing fees. Balance this financial plan with your available financial resources.

Entry-Level Salaries

Recognize that a career known for having high earning potential may initially start out at a much lower income than you would expect. Know what you can reasonably expect to earn as an entry-level salary when you begin your career. O*Net provides a search feature under Workforce Characteristics, Wage & Employment Trends, and State Wages that shows income levels by location and nationwide. Use the search criteria to look at a specific geographical area and consider the lower end of the bell curve instead of the median or high end. The income listed under the column "Annual Low (10 percent)" should be the income projection when you are first entering the workforce.

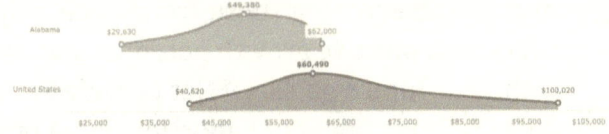

O*Net, State Wage Search Feature

Another option is to use the research strategy of looking at online job postings, as they often state a position's salary range in conjunction with experience and education levels. This can give you a clearer sense of what compensation is realistic in your desired field.

Growth Potential

Research and evaluate the potential for salary growth. Important factors to consider include career advancement, promotions, skill development, and industry trends, all of which can contribute to salary increases over time. Staying informed about industry trends that could impact compensation is essential. Additionally, recognize that some careers and industries offer more rapid advancement and/or higher earning potential.

Labor Market

Understanding the demand for professionals in a career or industry is essential for making informed decisions. Economic conditions, labor market trends, and emerging technologies can impact salary levels and job opportunities. High demand for specific skill sets often leads to competitive salaries and better career prospects, while low demand or oversaturation can limit opportunities, job stability, and earning potential. Researching these trends can help you identify careers with positive growth potential and salaries that align with your future goals. O*Net provides valuable data from the U.S. Department of Labor, including projected growth, job openings, wages, and employment trends. By exploring statistics on median wages, local wages, projected job growth, and state-specific trends, you can gain insights into the labor market and make informed career choices. The interactive tools for State and Local Wages are particularly helpful for understanding wage ranges by location.

	In Alabama:		In the United States:	
Employment (2020)	910 employees	Employment (2022)	123,400 employees
Projected employment (2030)	970 employees	Projected employment (2032)	124,100 employees
Projected growth (2020-2030)	7%	Projected growth (2022-2032)	1% Little or no change
Projected annual job openings (2020-2030)	100	Projected annual job openings (2022-2032)	13,000

O*Net, State Trends Search Feature

To continue your research use O*Net and/or job search engines to find current job postings in areas where you would consider living. Consider the following questions:

- How many job postings are available?

- What education, experience, and skills are required for qualified candidates?

- What companies are hiring?

- What is the advertised salary?

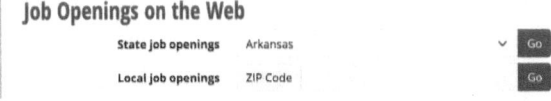

Job Openings on the Web

| State job openings | Arkansas | Go |
| Local job openings | ZIP Code | Go |

You may also want to consider the global perspective of the career field. In today's interconnected world, having a global mindset and understanding international trends can be advantageous. Also, understand how technological advancements and innovations may affect specific career fields. Embracing technology and being tech-savvy can enhance competitiveness in the labor market. This research can be done through a variety of means, depending on what information and field you are researching. Some options include:

- Academic databases including research papers, articles, and journals

- Industry reports, such as McKinsey & Company, Deloitte Insights, PwC and KPMG

- International organizations and think tanks, such as the World Economic Forum, United Nations, International Labor Organization, and Organization for Economic Co-operation and Development

- Global business news outlets, such as The Financial Times, The Economist, Harvard Business Review, TechCrunch, and Wired

- Professional associations (specific to the career field)

Compensation Packages

It is important to be aware of and consider the total compensation package beyond base income. Variables to consider may include bonuses, health insurance, benefits, retirement plans and contributions, and other perks offered by potential employers. These extras can significantly impact your total compensation. Carefully evaluate the benefits package offered by potential employers, and be aware of industry norms and trends.

Childcare Expenses

If you have children or plan to have children, another financial factor to consider is childcare expenses. Take into account the schedule and time demands of your career, as well as your childcare needs. Research and evaluate the costs of different childcare options to determine how they will impact your budget and career plans.

RETURN ON INVESTMENT

The following suggestions are intended to help you gain a comprehensive understanding of the costs associated with the training and education required for different career paths. Doing so will allow you to reasonably estimate the return on your investment of time and money.

Determining the cost of a degree involves considering various factors to accurately calculate the total cost of pursuing a career. Different education paths come with varying costs. Consider each career option and identify its specific training and education requirements. If applicable, know exactly what type of degree(s), license(s), or certification(s) are required. If the necessary education involves internships or practical training, take into account any associated costs, such as travel, accommodation, or work-related expenses. Some professions may also have ongoing membership fees or certification renewal costs. If your career requires continuous professional development or continuing education, estimate the costs of courses, workshops, or certifications throughout your career. Calculate all associated expenses, including tuition, living costs, loss of income, and student loans. Finally, compare the costs of training and education with the potential increase in earnings over the course of your career. This total will give you an estimate of the return on your financial investment in relation to your training and education.

Tuition

Research the tuition costs and fees associated with the training and education programs you are considering. This information should be easily accessible through the official websites of universities, colleges, or training institutions, providing accurate and up-to-date details on the costs. Estimate the cost of books, study materials, and supplies required. Consider whether digital resources or used books could help reduce costs. Compare the potential cost differences between online and on-campus programs. Additionally, note the expected duration of the required training and education, and compute the final costs based on the time it should take you to finish and begin employment.

Living Expenses

Calculate your living expenses, including rent, food, transportation, utilities, and any other known costs. If your training and education require you to relocate to a different city or country, research the cost of living in that location. Estimate the cost of necessary technology for your studies, such as a laptop, software, or specialized tools required for your field.

Loss of Income

Consider whether it is feasible for you to work full- or part-time during your studies. Learning how to balance part-time employment with your academic commitments can help cover some living expenses while you are in school. Many vocational programs offer paid training. Explore internships that provide hands-on experience in your field of study, some of which offer financial compensation (either as a stipend or hourly wages). Calculate the opportunity cost of pursuing training or education, especially if it involves leaving the workforce. Estimate the potential income you might forgo during the period of time you are in school.

Student Loans

Student loans are often available to students while they are pursuing their education, covering both the cost of schooling and living expenses. If you plan to take out student loans, it is vital to research the terms, interest rates, and repayment plans. Be cautious about accumulating excessive student loan debt. Evaluate the impact of student loan debt on your financial future and goals. Understand the long-term effects of student loans on your finances. Also, be aware of student loan forgiveness programs that might be available.

Tuition Assistance

Many avenues are available for receiving additional financial assistance to cover all or part of the costs of schooling, including employers, government programs, and other sources. Often, employers offer financial assistance to current employees pursuing further education.

If you are already employed, inquire about employer tuition assistance programs and explore paid training opportunities. Some states sponsor career pathway programs that can pay for technical education or short-term certificate programs, typically in exchange for a commitment to work in the state for a specified period of time. Additionally, some programs offer loan repayment in exchange for working in a certain field for a set period. The military offers tuition reimbursement programs that can cover up to 100 percent of tuition in exchange for a period of active duty service. This can apply to licensing and technical training programs, as well as undergraduate and advanced degrees.

Explore both need-based and merit-based opportunities to help offset the cost of education. Many schools use the Free Application for Federal Student Aid (FAFSA) to determine eligibility for need-based scholarships and grants. Higher education institutions that use FAFSA can offer federal, state, and institutional grants, scholarships, and loans.

Also, explore outside need-based and merit-based opportunities, such as scholarships and grants not administered through the educational institution. The counselors in your high school career center and the financial aid office at your college might be able to help you find outside scholarships and grants you can apply for. Carefully review the terms and conditions of all scholarships and grants, as some may have specific requirements that must be met to continue qualifying for renewal and/or to avoid repayment.

Get to Work

Think about what you have learned about financial realities of the cost of living, income, and return on investment. Ask yourself, "Does pursuing this career make financial sense?" Decide which financial factors matter the most to you when considering potential career choices—cost of living, income, return on investment, or a combination. (*Career Compass Workbook*, pages 15–17.)

- What income do you require to live the kind of life you envision for yourself?

- What is the earning potential and employability for careers on your Maybe List?

- Does the cost of training and education make financial sense for you given the career's earning potential (ROI)?

Check-in

Evaluating the financial aspects of potential career paths is a crucial step in making an informed decision about your future. Understanding the cost of living, income expectations, and the return on investment for the time and money spent preparing for a career can help you assess whether a particular path aligns with your financial goals and long-term stability. By carefully weighing these factors, you can choose a career that not only fits your strengths, interests, values, but also supports your financial needs and goals.

Chapter Eleven

Qualifications

This chapter's suggestions for career research will help you discover the qualifications for careers you are interested in pursuing. By gathering this information, you will be better equipped to make informed decisions about your career choices. This research can also help you create a detailed and intentional Career Plan once you've made a definitive choice.

Before you begin any career path, it is essential to understand three practical and important job requirements: education, experience, and skills. Knowing what is required in each of these areas will help you plan how to transition from where you are now to successful employment in your chosen career, in the most efficient way possible. When you clearly understand what education, experience, and skills are needed, you will be less likely to waste time, money, or effort, or face unexpected detours while pursuing your career.

Get Ready to Work!

Focus on what it takes to become qualified for the careers you're considering. For each option on your Maybe List, ask: What education, experience, and skills are required? Consider the various educational options available to gain the necessary qualifications/credentials for each career possibility. Then, evaluate how your current qualifications compare. Where are the gaps and what steps will you need to take to close them? (*Career Compass Workbook*, pages 18–19).

This research and reflection will help you build a clear and realistic Career Plan in the next phase of your journey.

EDUCATION

You want to know exactly how much education and training you are willing and able to pursue during your career preparation. It is also important to identify the specific level of education and training required to successfully enter a career field. Compare your willingness and ability to obtain education and training with the prerequisites of a career to assess compatibility.

Learn from credible sources the specific training, education, and/or certifications required for the careers on your Maybe List. On O*Net, under Experience Requirements, the section Job Zone identifies the amount of preparation, education, related experience, and job training for every career in their database.

Experience Requirements

Job Zone

Title	Job Zone Three: Medium Preparation Needed
Education	Most occupations in this zone require training in vocational schools, related on-the-job experience, or an associate's degree.
Related Experience	Previous work-related skill, knowledge, or experience is required for these occupations. For example, an electrician must have completed three or four years of apprenticeship or several years of vocational training, and often must have passed a licensing exam, in order to perform the job.
Job Training	Employees in these occupations usually need one or two years of training involving both on-the-job experience and informal training with experienced workers. A recognized apprenticeship program may be associated with these occupations.
Job Zone Examples	These occupations usually involve using communication and organizational skills to coordinate, supervise, manage, or train others to accomplish goals. Examples include hydroelectric production managers, desktop publishers, electricians, agricultural technicians, barbers, court reporters and simultaneous captioners, and medical assistants.
SVP Range	(6.0 to < 7.0)

The next section, Training and Credentials, has search features that will produce a list for the categories of State Training, Local Training, Certifications, and State Licenses.

The State and Local Training searches produce a list of programs and schools, with hyperlinks to their affiliate websites for certifications and state licenses.

The Certifications search produces a list of nationwide certifications, along with hyperlinks and the associated certifying organizations.

The State License search produces a list of license titles with hyperlinks and the associated agency for each state.

Use the hyperlinks to quickly reference and search each program and school's website. While researching the program, learn about their completion/graduation requirements, possible prerequisites, the amount of time it takes to complete, and all associated costs for the program.

Make sure to thoroughly research all prerequisite requirements early in your training and education, especially when your career choice requires advanced degrees, certifications, or licenses. Some careers may require acceptance into specific schools or programs, and not being admitted could require you to adjust your plans. Poor research and planning can delay acceptance into programs, lead to additional time spent applying to alternate schools, or result in not meeting qualifications to proceed with your required education. This can cause unnecessary stress and frustration, as well as additional time and monetary costs that could have been avoided.

Research several schools to compare costs and available programs. Look into tuition fees, financial aid opportunities, and any additional costs like textbooks or supplies. Evaluate the quality of the programs by reviewing the curriculum, faculty qualifications, internships, and career support services offered. By comparing these factors, you can make a more informed decision about which school offers the best value and aligns with your career goals, ensuring you choose a program that provides the skills and opportunities needed for your future.

EXPERIENCE

Experience is a broad topic that can be broken down into three subcategories: experience required, related experience, and work experience. In addition to education and training requirements, it is also important to research what experience is necessary to work in a career.

One of the easiest ways to ascertain the experience requirements for a specific career is to search for that position on job search engines like Indeed (indeed.com), Monster (monster.com), or CareerBuilder (careerbuilder.com). Under current job postings, you will often find an "Experience Required" section that lists the education, training, credentials, specific work experience (sometimes specified by a time frame), and skills needed to qualify a candidate for consideration.

LinkedIn (linkedin.com) can also provide valuable insights into the experience required to work in certain careers. By researching profiles of people currently working in the career you are interested in, you can review their work history posted on their profile. Tracing their career paths can inform you about the direction you will need to take if you choose to pursue that career.

Often, when a person is seeking employment, they can feel frustrated if they are not qualified to apply for positions they want due to a lack of experience. Many times, the experience listed in job postings is non-negotiable. However, related experience can sometimes qualify a candidate for a position. Transferable skills from education and other work experiences can occasionally serve as a substitute, or you can plan ahead to gain the necessary experience.

It's not only helpful, but also very important for individuals to have a wide variety of work experience. Many employers are looking for candidates with work experience more so than schooling in today's work environment. It is highly suggested to gain work experience, even if the work experience is in a field you may not be considering as a longstanding career choice. This experience shows your character and provides invaluable insight and practical knowledge which can influence prospective employer decisions. Work experience is a key way to learn about yourself—what you enjoy, what you are good at, where you thrive, and what drives you crazy, among other things. It also provides first-hand insights into different industries, roles, and work environments, which can help clarify your career goals. Work experience allows for exploration, helping you uncover your interests and preferences, discover what types of work you enjoy, and identify areas where you excel.

It is also important to recognize that theory and classroom learning only goes so far. Work experience exposes individuals to the practical aspects of a job or industry, giving them a real-world understanding of the day-to-day responsibilities of that job.

Work experience can provide valuable insights when it comes to important decisions regarding career choices. It helps individuals assess whether a particular career path aligns with their values, lifestyle preferences, and long-term career goals. The experience gained from work can also provide practical knowledge on where to obtain further education, and which opportunities or organizations offer the best training and experience to develop or refine the specific skills necessary for success.

Individuals should gain a variety of work and service experiences before deciding on and starting any education or training path. Volunteer or paid work experience, even if it is not directly in the career field you intend to pursue, will teach you a lot about yourself and your work preferences. Any job can provide valuable insights into what you enjoy, where you thrive, and what drives you crazy. Additionally, the on-the-job training you receive through work experience(s) can help you develop many transferable skills and abilities that will be attractive to future employers.

Too often, people regret their career choice once they finish their education and training to gain the necessary skills and qualifications and begin working in the field they had planned and prepared for. They often quickly learn that their lack of compatibility with the field could have been determined earlier through work experience and self-reflection. Without these insights, people may face regret that could have been prevented. They are then left with the difficult decision of how to proceed—stick with a career that doesn't meet their needs or start over and potentially spend more time and money transitioning into something else that now seems like a better fit.

SKILLS

Closely related to experience is the topic of skills. In fact, "skills" is often the language used in job postings when outlining employment qualifications. While gaining experience is important, it is equally essential to focus on developing the specific skills that will prepare and qualify you for success in your future career.

Skills can encompass four different types of skills you need to be aware of during your career research—soft skills, transferable skills, hard skills, and job related/job specific skills. Having the right technical abilities and soft skills, such as communication, problem-solving, and team-work, is critical for success in nearly every job. Whether through formal education, on-the-job training, or personal development, acquiring the right skill set can make you a more competitive candidate in the labor market.

It is important to identify the key skills required for the career paths on your Maybe List, and actively seek opportunities to develop those skills. Reviewing job descriptions, conducting informational interviews, or connecting with professionals in your desired field can help you gain a clear understanding of the most valued skills for your career. You can't concentrate solely on experience without also developing the skill set that will prepare and qualify you for success in your future career. Be proactive in acquiring and refining these skills to ensure you are well-equipped to meet the demands of your future career.

Author's Note

Be honest with yourself about your education, work abilities, skill capabilities, and potential for growth. Ask yourself: Can I realistically develop and master the skills necessary to excel in this career? It is important to strike a balance between confidence and self-aware-ness—too much confidence can lead to underestimating the challenges ahead, while undervaluing your abilities can hold you back from pursuing opportunities that are well within reach. In my experience working

with clients and students, I see both extremes—those
who overestimate their preparedness, and those who
doubt their potential. Recognizing where you fall on
this spectrum and adjusting your mindset accordingly
is key to making informed, strategic, and realistic career decisions.

Get to Work

What have you learned about the necessary qualifications
for different career options?

- Use the *Career Compass Workbook* to record the
  specific job qualifications for the careers on your
  Maybe List, making sure to note education, experience, and skills (page 18).

- For each career, research multiple schooling options. Document the associated costs and expected
  time for completion. (*Career Compass Workbook*,
  page 19.)

Check-in

As you conduct your research into different career possibilities, imagine yourself living the life you envision with
that career. Consider not only the job itself but also the
time and effort it will take to become qualified and employable in that field. Picture yourself growing in the career
over time. Do you feel excitement, dread, or something in
between?

Chapter Twelve

Test Drives

The research you've done should have led you to several career possibilities worth serious consideration. But all the research up until this point has been theoretical. Theory is not enough; it's actually just the beginning! You should always get real-life experience before you commit to a career. Test-drive a career before you commit!

While learning through research—like the work you've done on yourself and the contemplation on career options on your Maybe List—valuable, hands-on experience can teach you even more. The best way to test-drive a career is to get a job in or near the field you're considering. For example, if you think you want to be a teacher, consider working as a teacher's aide. Or, if you're interested in becoming a graphic designer, try taking on freelance design projects or working as an assistant to a professional designer. Sometimes, what looks good on paper doesn't always live up to expectations in practice. Before making a final decision, be sure to test out your career ideas. If a job in the field isn't immediately available, there are other ways to gain experience, such as conducting informational interviews, participating in internships, job shadowing, volunteer opportunities, or mentorship programs. Use your personal and professional networks to gather as much information as possible before settling on your final career choice.

If you do decide to pursue the career field you've tested out, the experiences you gained—whether through internships, volunteer work, or other hands-on opportunities—will add significant value to your resume. Not only will you have gained practical skills, but it also demonstrates to potential employers that you have real-world experience and a genuine commitment to the field. These experiences can give you a competitive edge and make you stand out when applying for jobs or further educational opportunities.

Get Ready to Work!

Consider the various options available to gain real-life experience in the careers you are interested in.

INFORMATIONAL INTERVIEWS

An informational interview is a conversation in which a person seeks insights into a career path, an industry, a company, or general career advice from someone with experience and knowledge in their areas of interest. Informational interviews are often casual and candid conversations where both parties focus simply on acquiring and sharing knowledge. The professional being interviewed is doing a favor by providing information; therefore, it is important to be mindful of informational interview etiquette. (See the Appendixfor guidance on Informational Interviews, including Etiquette and Sample Questions.)

JOB SHADOWING

Job shadowing provides insight into a job that goes beyond what can be gained from reading about it or conducting research. Job shadowing involves spending time with someone who performs the job you are interested in, allowing you to observe, ask questions, and learn new skills. Some of the benefits of job shadowing include observing multiple career possibilities, learning about organizational or job culture, getting a glimpse into a job's perks and challenges, and having a safe space or person to ask questions.

INTERNSHIPS

An internship is a great introduction to an industry or role you may want to pursue. Internships are typically arranged through an educational counselor who can help match you with a company that fits your career goals. Understanding the benefits of doing an internship can help you decide if this is the right course of action for you.

An internship is a hired introductory position for a defined period. Internships can be paid or unpaid, with the main purpose being for the intern to gain experience. You typically apply for an internship during your undergraduate or graduate studies in your chosen field and then work for a company for one or more months, either full-time or part-time. You might work as an intern over the summer or during a semester or quarter while taking classes. Some internships allow you to receive college credit upon completion. Though less common, some internships are also available to high school students.

Internships can help you gain valuable work experience, fulfill college requirements, and provide material to add to your resume. They introduce you to many aspects of full-time employment while allowing you to explore your interests and form your personal career goals.

VOLUNTEER

Sometimes, no internship programs are available, but it never hurts to ask if you can volunteer! Volunteering may provide you with more flexibility in terms of the amount of time required, while still giving you the opportunity to learn and gain experience.

MENTORSHIP PROGRAMS

Mentorship programs offer personalized guidance and support from experienced professionals, helping students navigate their educational and career journeys with greater confidence. These programs may be available through schools (high school or college) or as part of community organizations or businesses.

Get to Work

Think about ways for you to get real life insights into the careers you are considering. What methods can you use to gain real-life experience in the careers you are considering for your future? (*Career Compass Workbook*, page 20.)

- Informational Interviews/Job Shadowing: Who do you know that works in the careers you are considering? Reach out to them and ask if you can interview them about their job, and/or shadow them for a few hours, day, or a week.

- Internships/Volunteer Work: Research companies or organizations in your field of interest and apply for internships or volunteer positions.

- Mentorship Programs: Find programs in your area.

Check-in

Take opportunities to gain real life knowledge and experience in order to make informed career decisions. Exploring different career options in various ways can help you better understand the day-to-day realities of each role. Hands-on experience can clarify whether careers align with your strengths, interests, values, and goals. It also provides a deeper perspective that cannot be gained from research alone. Real-world experience bridges the gap between theory and practice, helping you choose a career that truly fits you.

Chapter Thirteen

Reflect & Analyze

Author's Note

When it comes to choosing or evaluating a career, I often use the analogy of dating or choosing a romantic partner. Some people believe there's one perfect partner out there for them—a soulmate. I believe that, even if that's true for relationships, when it comes to careers, there are many great matches for each person. So, don't get stuck thinking you need to find the one perfect career. If you wait for that ideal career match ("soulmate"), you might miss out on some truly amazing opportunities.

And even if there is one perfect career match, does that mean the relationship will be flawless? Aren't there always small annoyances, compromises, or concessions in every relationship? (By both parties?!) The same holds true for careers.

Keep this perspective in mind during this chapter.

Some people become overwhelmed, anxious, even para-lyzed when choosing a career path. They put pressure on themselves that they have to find the perfect job, as if there's only one career that could make them happy and fulfilled. I want to challenge this belief and propose to you that there are many, many great career fits for everyone. Your career choice doesn't need to be a 100% perfect match. (Is anyone completely happy with every single ele-ment of their job? No! There are always some annoyances, concessions, and compromises.)

Deciding if a career is a good fit for you isn't about finding perfection. It is about evaluating what matters most to you. Then you can confidently choose something that comes really close, without compromising what matters the most to you.

(Also, just like choosing a romantic partner, you don't need to settle for something that's convenient but not actu-ally well-suited to you. It is a good idea to be a little choosy!)

All the research you have done will help you get a clearer picture of your career options and see if you can picture yourself in a particular role. Research can be the bridge between "maybe" and making a decision about your future career path. It helps you make informed decisions. It is how you can not just learn about a career but also evaluate if it is a good fit for you.

Unfortunately, there is no simple formula to compute your research and determine which careers are the best fits for you, as there are too many personal variables to weigh and consider. Go back to your notes throughout the *Career Compass Workbook*. After completing Parts 1 and 2 of this book and the workbook, you now have a better understanding of your story and personal considerations. It's time to compare what you know about yourself to all the career research you've done and assess how each ca-reer possibility aligns with you. To help with this process, create a list of your most important career considerations to measure and gauge your decision-making, ensuring you stay focused on what truly matters to you.

Get Ready to Work!

Keep an open mind as you reflect on and analyze various career options. Remember, choosing a career path isn't about finding one perfect match; there will be many great options that align with your strengths, interests, values, and goals. As you explore your options, you should also begin identifying careers that are not a good fit for you. This process will help you narrow down your Maybe List.

Think about ways to implement a system to track your level of interest in each career, as your perspectives may evolve throughout the research process. Use the *Career Compass Workbook*, pages 21–22, to document your research on the careers from your Maybe List and evaluate it compared to your specific career considerations.

STRENGTHS

Consider how each career option complements your personality. How you approach this will depend on which, if any, personality assessments you've taken (Chapter 6). Whatever career or personality assessment you utilize can serve as a tool to evaluate your unique characteristics against potential career choices.

While researching a career, look at its typical job duties, responsibilities, required skills, educational qualifications, work environment, and lifestyle factors. For initial research, use online resources like O*Net and My Next Move. Critically compare your own personality traits and preferences with the characteristics and demands of each career. Evaluate how well your personality traits align with the day-to-day tasks, work environment, temperament, obstacles, and challenges associated with each career.

Also, reflect on all your past work experiences, such as academic projects, extracurricular activities, internships, volunteer work, or jobs. This will help you identify how your personality meshes with work tasks, environments, and responsibilities that you enjoyed or excelled in (as well as identifying the opposite, which can be just as useful). These insights can inform and shape your career exploration and decision-making process.

INTERESTS

Interests are the most common variable people consider when contemplating career options because they can be the easiest to articulate and identify. However, "interest" can sometimes be a limiting term for some individuals—what might start as an interest for some people may actually be a passion! Be cautious in assuming that just because you have a strong interest or passion, it automatically means it will be a good career fit for you. While interests and passions are fantastic to consider, you could be limiting yourself if you focus solely on these variables. The truth is, you do not have to have a strong interest or passion in a career to experience enjoyment and satisfaction.

Balance interests and passions with practicality. While interest and passion can be crucial for job satisfaction, it is essential to ensure that your career choices align with your future goals. Recognize that for some people, working in an area they are passionate about can diminish or tarnish their love for it. Also, consider the reality that interests and passions can change over time and might fade. As new interests and passions emerge, does that mean you will need to shift or alter your career path? This belief could lead to unnecessary career changes.

If it doesn't make sense to pursue your interests or passions professionally, consider other variations, such as maintaining them as hobbies or side jobs. Other practical factors to balance with interests and passions include variables like ability, salary, job availability, labor market demand, and education requirements.

VALUES

When navigating career choices, it is essential to consider both personal and professional values. Personal values, such as work-life balance, ethical beliefs, and passions, influence long-term job satisfaction and alignment with your overall life goals. Professional values, including integrity, collaboration, and career growth opportunities, impact your ability to thrive in a work environment and contribute meaningfully to your field. Choosing a career that aligns with both sets of values helps ensure fulfillment, reduces the risk of burnout, and enhances your overall sense of purpose and achievement. Ultimately, a career that reflects your values is more likely to lead to sustained success and happiness.

O*Net provides a search tool to browse by six different Work Values: Achievement, Independence, Recognition, Relationships, Support, and Working Conditions. Three of these values are also listed under Workforce Characteristics for each career page.

Browse by Work Values

Work values are global aspects of work that are important to a person's satisfaction. Select a work value to discover occupations that reinforce the work value.

☑ Achievement
Occupations that satisfy this work value are results oriented and allow employees to use their strongest abilities, giving them a feeling of accomplishment. Corresponding needs are Ability Utilization and Achievement.

☑ Independence
Occupations that satisfy this work value allow employees to work on their own and make decisions. Corresponding needs are Creativity, Responsibility and Autonomy.

☑ Recognition
Occupations that satisfy this work value offer advancement, potential for leadership, and are often considered prestigious. Corresponding needs are Advancement, Authority, Recognition and Social Status.

☑ Relationships
Occupations that satisfy this work value allow employees to provide service to others and work with co-workers in a friendly non-competitive environment. Corresponding needs are Co-workers, Moral Values and Social Service.

☑ Support
Occupations that satisfy this work value offer supportive management that stands behind employees. Corresponding needs are Company Policies, Supervision: Human Relations and Supervision: Technical.

☑ Working Conditions
Occupations that satisfy this work value offer job security and good working conditions. Corresponding needs are Activity, Compensation, Independence, Security, Variety and Working Conditions.

As part of your career research, compare the work values of different careers to your own values. If the job you choose conflicts with your personal values, it can lead to unhappiness and discontentment over time. For example, if you value work-life balance but end up in a high-stress job with long hours, you may feel frustrated and overwhelmed. Similarly, if you value creativity and find yourself in a rigid, rule-bound environment, it can be hard to stay motivated or satisfied.

Also examine the work culture, expectations, and values of each different career to assess whether they align with your values. This will allow you to make a more informed decision and help ensure that the career path you choose will lead to fulfillment rather than dissatisfaction.

GOALS

Reflect on the vision you had for your future when you first started this book. The questions you asked yourself about what you want—whether it's where you live, the lifestyle you desire, or the time you wish to spend with family and friends—remain just as important today. Your career, while a significant part of your life, is only one piece of a much bigger puzzle. Now, think about how the career paths you've explored can align with the future you imagined. Can the careers you're considering help shape the life you desire? Remember, your future is yours to create, and every decision you make, big or small, is part of building the life you envision. Keep those visions in mind as you move forward, and continue to ask yourself how your career fits into that picture, adapting as needed to stay true to what matters most to you.

ANYTHING ELSE?

In addition to strengths, interests, values and goals, you have explored a range of other factors that can play a crucial role in making your career decision. Weigh these considerations as needed into your decision making process.

Get to Work

Reflect and analyze the career research to determine which careers align with who you are—weighing your strengths, interests, values, goals, and anything else that is important for you to consider when making your decision.

- What specific career considerations do you want—or need—to keep in mind when making your decision? How would you evaluate or rank your career options based on each of the areas you've identified as important? Consider using a strategic method, such as a Decision Matrix (*Career Compass Workbook*, page 22), to compare and assess your options objectively.

- Which careers, if any, have you eliminated from your list?

- Which careers are you still interested in?

Check-in

While reflecting and analyzing during your career research, you should have been able to narrow down and
prioritize which careers on your Maybe List interest you
the most. Which careers stand out to you?

Part 3: Recap
Explore Options

Exploring your career options should be a thoughtful and thorough process. Carefully consider the factors that matter most to you and systematically research career options to make a well-informed career decision. Remember, career decisions are personal and can evolve over time because of various factors, so remain open to reassessing your options periodically.

Your career research should include investigations into finances, qualifications, and test drives. All of these factors then need to be weighed against what you know about yourself to determine if you think your career options are a good long-term fit for you.

Part 4 - Create a Career Plan

Chapter Fourteen

Mapping Plans

A common saying is: "A goal without a plan is just a wish." This saying holds true, especially when it comes to your career journey. Once you've decided on your career goal, it is time to map out plans for how you will achieve it. Without a well-defined plan, your goal remains a distant wish, a mere hope that things will fall into place on their own. To take control of your future, you must actively map out a written Career Plan. Doing so will dramatically increase the likelihood of success, providing you with clear direction and purpose as you move forward.

A Career Plan is not just about writing down your goal; it involves outlining the specific steps needed to achieve it. Each step should be informed by all the research and self-assessment you have done up until this point. All the time you've spent understanding yourself and exploring different career paths will now be used to construct an actionable plan. All your hard work will pay off as you strategically map out the path to your desired future.

A Career Plan is not a rigid, one-time exercise; it is an evolving roadmap that should change along with your personal and professional growth. Don't be afraid to shift your goals as your priorities and circumstances change—this flexibility will help you stay motivated and resilient as you pursue long-term success.

As you create various Career Plans, consider which plans promote ongoing skill development and growth. In today's fast-changing world, it is crucial to keep learning and improving. Be open to adjusting your goals as you progress, gain new experiences, and learn more about yourself and the industry.

Get Ready to Work!

Consider the careers on your Maybe List and think about which careers you would like to map out. As you create Career Plans for those careers, reflect on the factors that will guide you toward making a more informed and intentional decision. Consider how each plan aligns with your strengths, interests, values, and goals. Use these insights to help you move forward with confidence. (The Career Plan template is on pages 23–24 in the *Career Compass Workbook*.)

CAREER PLAN

A Career Plan serves many purposes once you have made a decision on your career. A Career Plan helps you make focused and informed decisions about your education, experience, and skill development. It ensures that your choices align with your long-term objectives, giving you a clearer sense of direction as you navigate your career path.

A Career Plan serves as a guide for your professional development. It outlines what you need to acquire or develop in order to advance in your chosen field, making your progression intentional and strategic.

A Career Plan allows you to manage your time more effectively. By identifying your priorities, you can focus on tasks and activities that contribute to your specific goals, while minimizing distractions or actions that don't align with your career.

A Career Plan clarifies your professional goals and aspirations, helping you define what success looks like for you. It provides a clear set of objectives to strive for, guiding your decisions and actions along the way.

While a Career Plan provides structure, it is important to embrace flexibility. Unexpected opportunities or changes may arise, and being adaptable allows you to seize these possibilities while staying true to your overall vision. Career Plans should evolve with your circumstances, aspirations, and as opportunities change over time. Regularly reexamine your plan to ensure it remains relevant.

Smart Goals

A Career Plan should be created using the SMART Goals method, a proven and widely-used approach for setting clear, actionable, and achievable objectives. SMART goals help break down both short- and long-term career aspirations into manageable steps, making it easier to track progress and stay motivated. By using this method, you can turn your big ideas into actionable tasks, ensuring that each step you take brings you closer to your ultimate career goal. SMART stands for:

S - Specific
Avoid: Avoid vague or broad objectives.
Ask yourself: What exactly do I want to achieve? Who needs to be involved? Where will this happen?

M - Measurable

Avoid: Objective that can not be quantified or tracked.
Ask yourself: How will you know when the goal is accomplished?

A - Achievable

Avoid: Unrealistic or unobtainable outcomes give your skills, resources, or circumstances.
Ask yourself: Is this goal feasible given my current situation?

R - Relevant

Avoid: Goals that do not contribute to your overall life and career plans.
Ask yourself: Does this goal make sense in the context of my long-term aspirations? Will it move me closer to the career I desire?

T - Time-Bound

Avoid: No deadline or a goal that can easily be postponed.
Ask yourself: When do I want to achieve this goal? What are the key deadlines or milestones I need to hit along the way?

Using SMART goals will help you stay focused, organized, and motivated as you work toward your career goals, allowing you to break down your larger vision into actionable, tangible steps. The SMART method creates a structured approach to reaching your career in three specific areas; qualifications (education, experience and skills), goals, and creating an action plan.

Education, Experience, Skills

During the career research you completed in Part 3, you identified the qualifications needed to be employable in the different career possibilities, including the education, experience, and skills required. Revisit those notes and create a list of all the education, experience, and skills needed to be employed in each career. Next, separate that list into what you already have and what you still need to acquire.

Goals

Examine the list of education, experience, and skills you need to acquire. Use these items to create Short-Term (0–2 years), Mid-Term (2–5 years), and Long-Term (5+ years) goals. This approach will help you map out a clear timeline for acquiring the necessary qualifications while ensuring that you stay on track toward your career objective.

It is important to recognize that achieving your career goals should not come at the expense of other areas of your life. To ensure a balanced and sustainable path, categorize these goals while considering the full spectrum of your life—education, work, and personal responsibilities. Consider how these goals will intersect with and impact your personal life, relationships, and overall well-being.

By integrating all aspects of your life into your goal-setting process, you create a realistic and achievable plan that is sustainable over the long term. Balance is key. It is not just about ticking off career milestones; it is about building a life that fosters growth in every area. By staying mindful of your broader goals and personal needs, you'll avoid burnout and ensure that your pursuit of professional success remains aligned with your overall well-being.

Identify which goals are more immediate and which are part of a longer-term trajectory. Balance short-term goals that can be achieved in the near future with long-term goals that contribute to your overarching career vision. This approach helps you create a sense of accomplishment while keeping you focused on the bigger picture. Achieving a balance between short-term wins and long-term aspirations will sustain your momentum and ensure steady progress.

Make sure these career goals align with your goals for your future. This consistency will enhance your motivation and satisfaction as you work toward achieving your objectives. Be realistic and remember that progress takes time. Celebrate your achievements along the way to maintain your momentum and keep from getting discouraged. With each small win, you'll build the confidence and determination needed to continue progressing toward your ultimate career goal.

Action Plan

Action Plan is where you break your larger career goals into smaller, manageable steps. These plans can be structured to suit your schedule—whether weekly, monthly, by semester, or yearly—depending on your personal circumstances and the career you have chosen. While creating your Action Plan, be sure to consider your Short-, Mid-, and Long-Term Goals. For each goal, develop a detailed action plan that outlines the specific steps, resources, and timeline needed to accomplish each objective. Don't hesitate to adjust these elements as needed to better align with your unique objectives.

Conscientiously apply the SMART goal principles to your Action Plan. Each element of your Action Plan should be Specific, Measurable, Achievable, Relevant, and

Time-Bound. Following this method helps you set realistic goals, stay on track, and remain accountable. It also helps you recognize when adjustments might be necessary. Knowing you have a structured plan in place can significantly boost your confidence and sense of control in your professional journey.

You might be tempted to skip creating an Action Plan, but don't give in to that urge! Skipping this step will limit your ability to track progress and stay focused. An Action Plan creates accountability, acting as a reminder of where you are now and where you want to go. It will serve as a roadmap for your decisions, especially when you encounter crossroads along your career path. By using an Action Plan, you can anticipate challenges, mitigate potential risks, and navigate obstacles with more strategic foresight.

Prioritize your goals based on their significance and impact on your overall career plan. If a goal feels too complex or overwhelming, break it down into smaller, manageable tasks or set a specific timeframe, such as creating an Action Plan for the upcoming semester. This approach makes the goal more achievable and allows you to make steady progress step by step. By balancing short-term wins with long-term aspirations, you'll stay motivated and maintain focus on your broader career vision.

Establish a Network

The topic of networking has been discussed extensively throughout this book; one of the most powerful tools you can have throughout your career journey is a solid network. Share your Career Plan, including your goals and Action Plan, with mentors, colleagues, family members, or friends, and actively seek their constructive feedback. External perspectives can provide valuable insights and help refine and improve your approach. Sharing your goals with your network not only helps you gain fresh ideas but also creates a sense of accountability, motivating you to stay on track.

If you have not already, consider setting networking goals as part of your Career Plan. Establishing and nurturing professional relationships can open doors to job opportunities, collaborations, and career advancement. Make time for networking and relationship-building activities, such as attending industry events, reaching out to potential contacts, and maintaining ongoing communication with established connections.

Review & Revise

A Career Plan is not static—it should be a living document that you regularly revisit. Take time to assess your progress, review the steps you have taken, and reevaluate your goals to ensure they are still aligned with your evolving aspirations. This regular check-in allows you to make necessary adjustments and stay focused on your path. Life and careers can take unexpected turns, so do not be discouraged if you find yourself off track or experience delays. It is completely normal to encounter setbacks. The key is to be flexible, reassess when needed, and readjust your approach. The most important thing is to keep moving forward, even if it is in smaller steps. Establishing a routine for these check-ins will also help you stay accountable to your goals and maintain momentum. In addition, it provides an opportunity to identify new opportunities or challenges that might arise, ensuring you're always adapting to any changes in your career trajectory.

Get to Work

Use your research to create a Career Plan for each career you are considering.

- Review the careers on your Maybe List. Choose a career and create a detailed Career Plan (*Career Compass Workbook*, pages 23–24).

- Reflect and analyze the Career Plan you created. In what ways does this career fit you? How does it align with what you know about yourself (strengths, interests, values, goals, etc.)?

- Repeat this process for as many careers on your Maybe List as necessary to determine the career you want to focus on moving forward.

Check-in

A career goal without a concrete plan is merely a wish. To turn your aspirations into reality, it is essential to develop a written Career Plan that outlines specific, actionable steps based on your research, self-assessment, and personal evaluations. Career Plans should reflect your current goals while also being flexible enough to evolve as you grow and learn throughout your career journey. While you draft multiple Career Plans, are you beginning to see a preferred career path?

Chapter Fifteen

Decision & Navigation

Making a career decision is not as simple as taking a test and then following a predetermined path. It's about putting all the pieces together and finding clarity through a process of exploration and reflection. For some, the decision might feel immediate and obvious—you start with an idea, work through exercises, and quickly feel confident in your choice. For others, the process might take a little longer, and that's okay too. Whether you've already found your path or need more time to refine your decision, this journey is about gaining confidence in your choice and ensuring that it's the right one for you. If you're still unsure, don't worry—sometimes the real clarity comes from more work and life experience.

Get Ready to Work!

Everything you've done—from the early reflections to the career exploration, assessments, and planning—has led you here. Now is the time to bring all those insights together. Revisit your answers, reflect on what you've learned about yourself, and use that clarity to make a confident, informed decision about your next step.

WEIGHING YOUR OPTIONS

When it's time to weigh your career options and make a decision, it is crucial to reflect on all the work you've done throughout the book. Start by revisiting where you worked on understanding yourself—your strengths, interests, values, and goals. You may have also taken various career assessments. Revisit any assessments you've done along the way to check for affirmations with your career options. These insights are the foundation for making an informed choice. Revisit your special considerations—your personal circumstances that need to be accounted for or accommodated in your career. Consider these factors and what role they play making your career choice.

Next, look back at your research where you explored various career options and reflected on how they align with what you know about yourself. Scan the Career Plans you outlined, and be honest with yourself as you integrate all these elements together. Reflect and analyze all your career options carefully.

A decision matrix (*Career Compass Workbook*, page 22) can help you analyze and evaluate your career research by assigning weights to your specific career considerations and scoring each option based on how well it meets those criteria. To use the decision matrix, list your identified career considerations on one axis, and career options on the other. Rate each career on a scale for how well it aligns with each consideration. You can use a visual method such as full circle, half circle, or empty circle to represent alignment (with the full circle could indicate a strong fit, a half circle a moderate fit, and an empty circle a poor fit) or a numeric scale (e.g., 1-4). Once complete, assess and compare your options and use the results to help you make a more informed and educated decision.

Take the time to discuss your options with someone who can offer valuable guidance—whether that's a family member, friend, mentor, advisor, or trusted colleague. A fresh perspective can help you see things you might have missed. By having these conversations, you'll be in a stronger position to make a well-rounded, confident decision, as you'll be able to consider different viewpoints and gather practical advice on your potential career paths. This discussion can help you assess the opportunities, challenges, and long-term growth in each field, giving you the clarity you need to choose the path that's right for you.

Struggling to Make a Decision

Making a career decision is never easy, and if you're still struggling to make a choice, know that you're not alone. It's completely normal to feel uncertain, but there are steps you can take to continue working through the process. If anxiety is clouding your judgment, seeking professional help—like a career coach or counselor—can provide clarity and support.

If you're feeling stuck, reexamine your options and do more research, but be careful not to use research as a form of procrastination. Some of the most common reasons people struggle with decisions include a lack of self-awareness, fear of making the wrong choice or failing, and pressure to find the "perfect" path.

Limited exposure to different career options or concerns about the labor market changing can add to confusion when making a career choice. Acknowledge these challenges, but don't let them paralyze you. Break the process down, focus on the factors you can control, and give yourself permission to make a decision—even if it's not the "perfect" one. You can always reevaluate and adjust your plans later.

Life Plans

Your career decision should align with your broader life plans and aspirations. Take a moment to reflect on your answer to the question in Chapter 4. How do you envision your future? Think more specifically about where you want to be in 5, 10, or even 15+ years. Having a clear and compelling vision for your future career is essential—it's the foundation upon which you'll build your goals. Consider the milestones you want to reach over the long term, both personally and professionally. These aspirations can shape the trajectory of your career and provide a roadmap for the short- and mid-term goals that lead you toward them. By defining your vision for the future, you'll create a sense of direction that helps you make decisions today with the bigger picture in mind, ensuring that each step brings you closer to the life and career you ultimately want.

Incorporating long-term thinking into your career planning allows you to navigate challenges with greater clarity and resilience. It's important to recognize that career paths are rarely linear. The journey to your ideal future may involve changes in direction, shifts in priorities, and even complete career pivots. It's completely normal to reassess your path as your personal and professional interests evolve over time. Rather than feeling discouraged by these changes, view them as opportunities to refine your vision and adapt to new possibilities. Understanding that it's okay to change careers or directions at any stage in life gives you the flexibility to explore new avenues without feeling tied to one choice. In fact, embracing this fluidity will help you remain adaptable and open to the opportunities that best align with your changing aspirations, ensuring that your career journey remains fulfilling and aligned with your long-term goals.

It's also important to remember that there should be no shame or guilt in changing career paths. Sometimes, a change is not only necessary but is the result of circumstances beyond your control—whether it's personal growth, changes in the economy, or shifts in your family situation. Rather than viewing a career change as a mistake or failure, try to see it as an opportunity for growth. Each shift or pivot is a reflection of your ability to adapt, learn, and pursue what truly aligns with your evolving goals and circumstances. Your career journey is unique, and it's important to honor the decisions you make along the way, knowing that each step, no matter how different from the last, is part of your growth and your bigger picture.

NAVIGATING YOUR CAREER

Once you have made a choice for your career and constructed a Career Plan, it is time to put your plan into action. Navigating your career will have its highs and lows. How you respond to both will determine your growth and success. You will experience moments of triumph, but also challenges and setbacks that may test your resolve. The key is to stay focused, remain adaptable, and keep refining your approach as you move forward. Remember, the journey is just as important as the destination, and each experience contributes to your personal and professional development.

Developing Grit

At the core of long-term career success is grit—the combination of passion and perseverance. Grit enables you to maintain a long-term perspective, even when faced with challenges or unexpected detours. Success is not about quick wins; it is about the steady, consistent effort toward your goals, despite setbacks or changes in direction.

Grit is built on several key principles. First, it involves having a long-term perspective. Success takes time, and the journey may be lengthy, but staying focused over the long haul will eventually lead to rewards. Grit also requires a willingness to work hard. It is often easier to sustain grit when your work aligns with your passions—when you enjoy what you do, perseverance feels more natural. However, grit also means putting in the effort, even when parts of the journey are less enjoyable, understanding that these challenges are a small price to pay for a greater long-term goal.

Another core aspect of grit is resilience. Setbacks are inevitable, and whether you face roadblocks or unexpected shifts, resilience helps you recover and keep moving forward. Grit also demands consistency. Even when progress feels slow or monotonous, sustained effort is key. Keep working day after day, even when things seem hard or unexciting.

Grit also requires adaptability. Career paths often evolve, and being flexible enough to adjust your goals when new opportunities or information arise is essential. Lastly, grit thrives on a growth mindset. Embrace challenges as opportunities to learn and view setbacks and mistakes as stepping stones for growth and discovery.

Success is not defined by sticking rigidly to a single plan but by your ability to stay committed, learn from setbacks, and adapt as necessary. No career journey is without detours. When you approach your goals with grit and adaptability, you will continue moving forward—no matter what obstacles arise. Stay focused on your long-term vision, embrace the learning process, and trust that persistence will eventually lead to success.

Challenges, Setbacks & Detours

Your road to success will not be without obstacles. At times you will feel like giving up or wonder if you are on the right path. You are familiar with the term grit, which means to stay committed even during tough moments. Instead of viewing challenges as barriers, see them as opportunities to demonstrate your determination and resolve. Learn from your mistakes, adjust your strategies, and keep going.

To harness your grit, set clear, achievable goals. Break larger objectives into smaller, manageable steps. This will help you maintain focus and motivation, even through difficult times. Time management is critical; dedicate consistent effort toward your goals, even when it feels like the progress is slow. Remember, passion alone is not enough—you need hard work and consistent effort to bring your goals to fruition.

Build a support system around you. Mentors, peers, and friends can provide advice and encouragement to help you stay on track. And as you achieve milestones, no matter how small, celebrate them. Recognizing your progress along the way will boost your motivation and remind you why you are on this journey in the first place.

Remember, not every moment in your career will be thrilling or exciting. At times, your work may feel routine or monotonous. But grit requires you to persevere through these periods. Even the most passionate careers require persistence through less glamorous tasks.

Failure is a normal part of the career exploration and journey process. If failure happens—when failure happens—do not let it discourage you. Use it as an opportunity to reflect, refine your approach, and move forward more effectively.

Course Corrections

Your career is not a fixed destination—it is a journey. Changing your mind about your career or adjusting your plan is natural, and sometimes even necessary. As you grow, so too will your understanding of what you want and need from your work. If something new sparks your interest or you realize a different career is a better fit, give yourself permission to pivot.

Please remember, changing your mind about your career is completely normal. Whether you are adapting your current plan or shifting to an entirely new path, staying committed and resilient will be key to your long-term success.

Career journeys are rarely linear. The path you initially set may change as your interests, goals, and circumstances evolve. It is important to periodically review and reassess your career plan, staying open to adjustments based on new experiences and opportunities. Flexibility is crucial, as unexpected detours—whether from external factors like economic shifts or personal reasons—are inevitable. The key is to maintain your resilience and stay committed to your goals.

Get to Work

Going back once again to the answers to the questions at the end of Chapter 4. Does my career choice align with what you are good at (strengths), what you enjoy (interests), what you value (core values), how you see your future (goals), and all your other important considerations? Make a decision on which career you want to pursue.

- Reflect on and analyze all your career options by comparing your research with your self-knowledge. If you're struggling to evaluate and compare your options, use a Decision Matrix (*Career Compass Workbook*, page 22) to help guide your process.

- Discuss your decision with trusted people from your network.

- Choose a career and set your plan in motion, anticipating that obstacles will arise along the way.

Check-in

Making a career decision is a deeply personal journey, and ultimately, it's your responsibility to take charge of your life and career. No one else can choose or manage your career path for you. Career management involves understanding yourself and what truly motivates you. As you encounter challenges—whether adjusting to unexpected setbacks or reevaluating your goals—remember that career management is an ongoing process. Stay proactive, flexible, and open to change as you navigate your journey. In the end, the successful navigation of your career path depends on you; the choices you make today will shape the future you create for yourself tomorrow.

Author's Concluding Message

In my work as an educator and career counselor, my goal is to help students and clients discover who they are, learn how to research prospective careers, and confidently choose and successfully map out a path that will efficiently lead them to their chosen destination. Becoming an author has not been an intentional goal in my career journey. I am not a writer; I am a teacher and counselor. My professional mission is to help others navigate their career choices by serving as a guide and advisor. Along the way, I have found many different paths to achieve this mission.

I teach. I am an adjunct professor at a community college, where I assist students in navigating their college experience and future careers, ensuring they have the tools to achieve both academic and professional success.

I provide counseling/coaching. I work privately with clients who seek one-on-one assistance in exploring their career options. My work with clients does not involve deciding for them or telling them which careers to pursue. Instead, sessions offer guidance and support as clients assess, explore, and plan for careers and futures that align with their skills, values, and aspirations. The goal is to empower clients to make their own informed decisions.

Now I've written this book, because taking a semester-long college class or participating in private career counseling is not a viable option for everyone. All of my efforts are aimed at achieving the same goal: help people gain the tools to understand themselves, explore career possibilities, and make informed and educated choices. I recognize that there is no single method for approaching this objective. To be effective, I must offer a variety of options to reach my audience.

Everyone who seeks help navigating their career choices deserves clear and effective guidance. Wisdom is asking for, seeking, and accepting assistance. I truly hope this book becomes a valuable tool that provides the help and guidance you need.

If you're interested, you can find additional resources and services I offer at vpcareerexploration.com.

Vicky Payne

Appendix

INFORMATIONAL INTERVIEWS

Objective

An informational interview provides you with a deeper understanding of the day-to-day realities of a job, the skills required, and the potential career paths available within a particular industry. Informational interviews can be invaluable during your career exploration to gain firsthand insights from professionals in your field of interest. These interviews should be used to gather this information to make more informed decisions about your career direction, determine if a specific field aligns with your personal interests and goals, and uncover potential challenges and opportunities that you may not have considered.

Etiquette

- Be polite and respectful when requesting an informational interview. Remember, you are not entitled to their time or advice.

- Acknowledge that the professional is doing you a favor by speaking with you, and express your gratitude.

- Be mindful of the time the professional is taking to answer your questions. A quality informational interview can typically be conducted in under 15 minutes.

- Avoid asking for personal information, such as salary or pay details. This is generally considered inappropriate.

- Come prepared with a list of thoughtful questions to guide the conversation.

- Express sincere thanks at the end of the interview. Follow up with a professional thank-you note or email to show your appreciation.

Sample Questions

- What has your career journey been like?

- What kind of educational background or training was required for this career?

- What are the most important skills needed to succeed in this position?

- What are some pros and cons of your job that someone should consider when exploring this field?

- What do you find most rewarding about this career? Or, what do you enjoy most about your job?

- What is your official job title?

- Can you describe a typical day or week at your job?

- What would you recommend someone do to prepare for a career in this field?

- What are the biggest challenges in this career?

- If you could give one piece of advice to someone just starting in this field, what would it be?

- What opportunities are there for advancement in this career field?

- How do you see this industry evolving in the next few years? Or, what are the most exciting developments in your field right now?

- Is there anything else you think would be important for me to know in order to make an informed decision about this career? Or, is there anything I should know or prepare for that may not be immediately obvious about this job?

About the Author

Vicky Payne is a Certified Vocational Rehabilitation Counselor and the founder of VP Career Exploration, a career counseling practice dedicated to helping individuals discover fulfilling professional paths. She specializes in administering career assessments and providing tools, resources, and courses that support self-discovery and informed career decision-making. Drawing on her experience working with people navigating career choices, exploring education options, and facing real-world workplace challenges, she is passionate about empowering individuals to uncover careers that align with who they are—and the kind of life they want to lead. Her approach emphasizes clarity, self-awareness, and a balanced view of passion, purpose, and practicality.

She also serves as an adjunct professor in the College Success Department at Johnson County Community College in Overland Park, Kansas, where she was honored with a nomination for the Lieberman Teaching Excellence Award.

Outside the classroom and her virtual career exploration practice, Vicky is a wife, mom to three young sons, and stepmom to an adult son. Each summer, she serves as the director of My City Allstars Overland Park, a multi-sport camp for youth. Her diverse career reflects her core belief: there's no single "right" career. Vicky finds joy and purpose in every role she takes on—and she's committed to helping others do the same.

Ways to connect:

- Website: vpcareerexploration.com

- LinkedIn: linkedin.com/company/ vp-career-exploration

- Facebook: facebook.com/VPCareerExploration

- Instagram: instagram.com/VPCareerExploration

- Email: info@vpcareerexploration.com